Stand Up For Freedom
Teachings on Liberty

Ezra Taft Benson

Compiled by Brian R. Mecham

2012 Ezra Taft Benson Society

All rights reserved.

ISBN: 1468180517
ISBN–13: 978-1468180510

To the seekers of truth.

"It was the struggle over free agency that divided us before we came here; it may well be the struggle over the same principle which will deceive and divide us again." (Ezra Taft Benson, "Be Not Deceived")

"... the truth shall make you free." (John 8: 32)

CONTENTS

Introduction — i

1. My People Are Destroyed for Lack of Knowledge — 1
2. A Plea to Strengthen Our Families — 5
3. The Book of Mormon Is the Word of God — 15
4. Beware of Pride — 22
5. The Twelfth Article of Faith — 30
6. The Constitution: A Heavenly Banner — 33
7. Stand Up For Freedom — 43
8. The Proper Role of Government — 62
9. Civic Standards for the Faithful Saints — 83
10. United States Foreign Policy — 91
11. Freedom and Free Enterprise — 110
12. Our Immediate Responsibility — 130
13. Christ and the Constitution — 149
14. Be Not Deceived — 157
15. Watchman, Warn The Wicked — 166
16. Not Commanded in All Things — 175
17. Righteousness Exalteth a Nation — 184
18. God, Family, Country — 193
19. I Testify — 199

INTRODUCTION

Throughout Ezra Taft Benson's years as an apostle, prophet and president of the Church of Jesus Christ of Latter-day Saints, he frequently added his voice of warning in regards to the consequences that face a sleeping and apathetic people. Let the words of this book serve as a reminder of the important teachings on liberty promoted by Ezra Taft Benson. Let us become aware of our awful situation as well as our responsibility and stewardship to ourselves, our families, communities and nation.

A few of the articles in this compilation have been updated. Nothing has been added to the words of Ezra Taft Benson but some details have been removed that relate more specifically to the day in which he spoke the words, except where those words were relevant to the principles being taught. In the days of Ezra Taft Benson the threat of communism was a much more real and open threat to freedom. Today that threat continues in the form of progressivism, Fabian socialism, etc. In other words, we're being led off the cliff slowly but surely and in ways that many do not even notice – like the proverbial frog in the pot of water slowly coming to a boil.

MY PEOPLE ARE DESTROYED FOR LACK OF KNOWLEDGE

My brethren and sisters, if the Lord will bless me I desire to say a few words about a most serious world–wide threat. In the Old Testament we read: "My people are destroyed for lack of knowledge." (Hosea 4:6.)

Thus spoke Hosea, the prophet. I take these words of warning as my text, "My people are destroyed for lack of knowledge."

As in Old Testament days we need knowledge today. We need to know our enemies. We must assess clearly and accurately the perils that face the free. At the same time we must assure ourselves of the knowledge which brings confidence and trust in our ability and that of our friends around the world to face the future—not in fear but with vigilance. From knowledge comes strength, and from strength comes the power to preserve freedom both at home and abroad.

Dedicated men have worked tirelessly to help the free world understand better the deadly world conflict between good and evil which is constantly going on.

We have an enormous responsibility here in the United States to help maintain peace and freedom and to push back the somber clouds of war–threats caused by international tensions.

The power of communism depends to a large extent on public ignorance. Knowledge is a dangerous thing – to totalitarian states; but knowledge is strength to a free people.

There are some fundamental facts which must never be overlooked, lest it be said of this our land, "My people are destroyed for lack of knowledge." (Hosea 4:6.)

We must never forget exactly what communism really is. Communism is far more than an economic system. It is a total philosophy of life – atheistic and completely opposed to all that we hold dear.

We believe in an all-wise Creator. Communism teaches that everything in existence came about as a result of ceaseless motion of the forces of nature.

We believe in the dignity of man. Communism holds that human beings are but graduate beasts. Hence communism does not hesitate to destroy those who stand in its way. The Russian communists in their rise to power liquidated millions of their fellow countrymen. The Chinese communists wiped out tens of millions—perhaps as many as 30 million.

We believe in a moral code. Communism denies innate right or wrong. As W. Cleon Skousen has said in his timely book, The Naked Communist: The communist "has convinced himself that nothing is evil which answers the call of expediency." This is a most damnable doctrine. People who truly accept such a philosophy have neither conscience nor honor. Force, trickery, lies, broken promises are wholly justified.

We believe in religion as a mode of life resulting from our faith in God. Communism contends that all religion must be overthrown because it inhibits the spirit of world revolution.

Earl Browder, a long-time leader of the Communist Party in the U. S. A. said, ". . . we Communists do not distinguish between good and bad religions, because we think they are all bad."

The major communist objective, make no mistake about it, is to destroy any society that adheres to the fundamentals of spiritual, economic, and political freedom – the integrity of man.

As the leading exponent of the free society, the United States is thus the primary target of Marxian–Lenin philosophy.

Internationally, communism seeks to isolate us from the rest of the free world. Here at home, communism ceaselessly pursues the disintegration of the American way of life. It strives to use education, science, literature, art, even the churches, to undermine our free society.

Suppose for a moment that this country fell under communist control. What would be the fruits of this calamity?

What can you and I do to help meet this grave challenge from a godless, atheistic, cruelly materialistic system—to preserve our God-given free way of life?

First, let us all prize the treasures we have in this country. This is a choice land – all of America – choice above all others. Blessed by the Almighty, our forebears have made and kept it so. It will continue to be a land of freedom and liberty as long as we are able and willing to advance in the light of sound and enduring principles of right.

Second, let us all do our part to stay free! Let us stand eternal watch against the accumulation of too much power in government. Here in our free land let us preserve a true climate in which man can grow.

Third, let us all reaffirm our patriotism, our love of country. Patriotism is more than flag-waving and brave words. It is how we respond to public issues. Let us rededicate ourselves as patriots in the truest sense.

Fourth, let us all help to build peace: True peace springs from within. Its price is righteousness, and to achieve righteousness we must so conduct ourselves individually and collectively as to earn the loyalty and devotion of other men.

Finally, let us all rededicate our lives and our nation to do the will of God. With each of you, I love this nation. It is my firm belief that the God of heaven guided the Founding Fathers in establishing it for his particular purposes. But God's purpose is to build free people of character, not physical monuments to their material accumulations.

Nations that truly love freedom love God. History is replete with examples of once powerful nations that have forgotten God. No nation ripened in iniquity can long endure. "Righteousness exalteth a nation: but sin is a reproach to any people." (Proverbs 14: 34)

We in this land have a rich heritage of freedom. It has rewarded us beyond our brightest dreams. The key to further progress – the key to national security – is the preservation of the initiative, vitality, energy, and resourcefulness of our people. Our material progress is merely a by–product of our freedom. Our God-given freedom, a basic principle of religious truth, is still the most powerful force on the face of the earth.

The people of the world long for peace. We know that knowledge of the enemy teaches us wariness and caution; we know too that we speak for millions of suppressed people, all those everywhere who want peace with human dignity.

May I conclude by saying that any system which deprives men of their free agency, which weakens the home and family, which depends on butchery for power, which denies all moral responsibility, which holds that man lives by bread alone, and which denies the existence of God, is of the devil. This is the communist philosophy.

Knowledge of the enemy and knowledge of ourselves give us the strength to fight the good fight for freedom and world peace.

May it never come to pass that "My people are destroyed for lack of knowledge," (Hosea 4:6) I humbly pray, in the name of Jesus Christ. Amen.

A PLEA TO STRENGTHEN OUR FAMILIES

As a people, we have three great loyalties: loyalty to God, loyalty to family, loyalty to country.

I come to you today with a plea to strengthen our families.

The Family Unit

It has been truly stated that "salvation is a family affair ... and that the family unit is the most important organization in time or in eternity."

The Church was created in large measure to help the family, and long after the church has performed its mission, the celestial patriarchal order will still be functioning. This is why President Joseph F. Smith said: "To be a successful father or a successful mother is greater than to be a successful general or a successful statesman..." and President McKay added: "When one puts business or pleasure above his home, he, that moment, starts on the downgrade to soul weakness."

And this is why President Harold B. Lee said only yesterday, "The Church must do more to help the home carry out its divine mission."

Temptations and Pitfalls

President Joseph Fielding Smith has stated that never "in the history of the Church have there been so many temptations, so many pitfalls, so many dangers, to lure away the members of the Church from the path of duty and from righteousness as we find today." (Take Heed to Yourselves, p. 127.) And he has also said: "This world is not growing better ... wickedness is increasing." (Ibid., p. 207.)

Never has the devil been so well organized, and never in our day has he had so many powerful emissaries working for him. We must do everything in our power to strengthen and safeguard the home and family.

The adversary knows "that the home is the first and most effective place for children to learn the lessons of life: truth, honor, virtue, self-control; the value of education, honest work, and the purpose and privilege of life. Nothing can take the place of home in rearing and teaching children, and no other success can compensate for failure in the home." (President David O. McKay, Family Home Evening Manual, 1968–69, p. iii.)

Undermining the Home

And so today, the undermining of the home and family is on the increase, with the devil anxiously working to displace the father as the head of the home and create rebellion among the children. The Book of Mormon describes this condition when it states, "And my people, children are their oppressors, and women rule over them." And then these words follow – and consider these words seriously when you think of those political leaders who are promoting birth control and abortion: "O my people, they who lead thee cause thee to err and destroy the way of thy paths." (2 Ne. 13:12.) And let me warn the sisters in all seriousness that you who submit yourselves to an abortion or to an operation that precludes you from safely having additional healthy children are jeopardizing your exaltation and your future membership in the kingdom of God.

Responsibility of Parents

Parents are directly responsible for the righteous rearing of their children, and this responsibility cannot be safely delegated to relatives, friends, neighbors, the school, the church, or the state.

"I appeal to you parents, take nothing for granted about your children," said President J. Reuben Clark, Jr. "The great bulk of them, of course, are good, but some of us do not know when they begin to go away from the path of truth and righteousness. Be watchful every day and hour. Never relax your care, your solicitude. Rule kindly in the spirit of the Gospel and the spirit of the priesthood, but rule, if you wish your children to follow the right path." Permissive parents are part of the problem.

False Educational Ideas

As a watchman on the tower, I feel to warn you that one of the chief means of misleading our youth and destroying the family unit is our educational institutions. President Joseph F. Smith referred to false educational ideas as one of the three threatening dangers among our Church members. There is more than one reason why the Church is advising our youth to attend colleges close to their homes where institutes of religion are available. It gives the parents the opportunity to stay close to their children; and if they have become alert and informed as President McKay admonished us last year, these parents can help expose some of the deceptions of men like Sigmund Freud, Charles Darwin, John Dewey, Karl Marx, John Keynes, and others.

Today there are much worse things that can happen to a child than not getting a full college education. In fact, some of the worst things have happened to our children while attending colleges led by administrators who wink at subversion and amorality.

Said Karl G. Maeser, "I would rather have my child exposed to smallpox, typhus fever, cholera, or other malignant and deadly diseases than to the degrading influence of a corrupt teacher. It is infinitely better to take chances with an ignorant, but pure-minded teacher than with the greatest philosopher who is impure."

Vocational education, correspondence courses, establishment in a family business are being considered for their children by an increasing number of parents.

Propagation of Atheism

The tenth plank in Karl Marx's Manifesto for destroying our kind of civilization advocated the establishment of "free education for all children in public schools." There were several reasons why Marx wanted government to run the schools. Dr. A. A. Hodge pointed out one of them when he said, "It is capable of exact demonstration that if every party in the State has the right of excluding from public schools whatever he does not believe to be true, then he that believes most must give way to him that believes least, and then he that believes least must give way to him that believes absolutely nothing, no matter in how small a minority the atheists or agnostics may be. It is self-evident that on this scheme, if it is consistently and persistently carried out in all parts of the country, the United States system of national popular education will be the most efficient and widespread instrument for the propagation of atheism which the world has ever seen.

After the tragic prayer decision was made by the Court, President David O. McKay stated, "The Supreme Court of the United States severs the connecting cord between the public schools of the United States and the source of divine intelligence, the Creator, himself." (Relief Society Magazine, December 1962, p. 878.)

Does that make any difference to you? Can't you see why the demand of conscientious parents is increasing the number of private Christian and Americanist oriented schools?

Today, Brigham Young University is the largest private school in the United States. Parents from far and near are looking to Brigham Young University as never before.

Supervision By Parents

Now, whether your child attends this type of school or not, it is important that you stay close to your children, daily review, if possible, what they have learned in school, and go over their textbooks.

President Joseph Fielding Smith has stated that in public schools you cannot get a textbook, anywhere that he knows of, on the "ologies" that doesn't contain nonsense. (Take Heed to Yourselves, p. 32.)

I know one noble father who reviews with his children regularly what they have been taught; and if they have been taught any falsehoods, then the children and the father together research out the truth. If your children are required to put down on exams the falsehoods that have been taught, then perhaps they can follow

President Joseph Fielding Smith's counsel of prefacing their answer with the words "teacher says," or they might say "you taught" or "the textbook states."

If your children are taught untruths on evolution in the public schools or even in our Church schools, provide them with a copy of President Joseph Fielding Smith's excellent rebuttal in his book *Man, His Origin and Destiny*.

Open Letter to School Principal

Recently some parents paid for space in a newspaper to run an open letter to the school principal of their son. The letter in part stated:

"You are hereby notified that our son, _____ is not allowed by his undersigned parents to participate in, or be subject to instruction in, any training or education in sex, human biological development, attitude development, self-understanding, personal and family life, or group therapy, or sensitivity training, or self-criticism, or any combination or degree thereof, without the consent of the undersigned by express written permission. ...

"We intend to retain and exercise our parental rights to guide our child in the areas of morality and sexual behavior without any interference or contradiction imposed by school personnel.

"[Our son] has been taught to recognize the format of sensitivity training, group therapy, self-criticism, etc., as it is being broadly applied, lowering the standards of morality and replacing American individual responsibility with the dependency on, and conformity to, the `herd consensus' concept of collectivism.

"He has been instructed to promptly remove himself from any class in which he is exposed to the aforementioned indoctrination and to report to us any such disregard of this letter."

Home Evening Program

The Lord knew that in the last days Satan would try to destroy the family unit. He knew that by court edict, pornography would be allowed to prosper.

How grateful we should be that God inspired his prophet over half a century ago to institute the weekly home evening program. This is the vanguard for getting parents to assume the responsibility of instructing their children. An increasing number of faithful Saints are holding more than one home evening a week and are adding to or deleting from the home evening manual as the Spirit dictates.

Designed to strengthen and safeguard the family, the Church home evening program (one night each week) is to be set apart for fathers and mothers to gather their sons and daughters around them in the home. Prayer is offered, hymns and other songs are sung, scripture is read, family topics are discussed, talent is displayed, principles of the gospel are taught, and often games are played and homemade refreshments served.

Now here are the promised blessings for those who will hold a weekly home evening:

"If the Saints obey this counsel, we promise that great blessings will result. Love at home and obedience to parents will increase. Faith will be developed in the hearts of the youth of Israel, and they will gain power to combat the evil influences and temptations which beset them." (First Presidency, April 27, 1915, Improvement Era, vol. 18, p. 734.)

Demoralizing Entertainment

Now what of the entertainment that is available to our young people today? Are you being undermined right in your home through your TV, radio, slick magazines, rock records? Much of the rock music is purposely designed to push immorality, narcotics, revolution, atheism, and nihilism, through language that often has a double meaning and with which many parents are not familiar.

Parents who are informed can warn their children of the demoralizing, loud, raucous beat of rock music, which deadens the senses and dulls the sensibilities—the jungle rhythm which inflames the savagery within.

Said President J. Reuben Clark, Jr.:

"I would have you reflect for a moment upon the fact that a tremendous amount of the modern art, of the modern literature and music, and the drama that we have today is utterly demoralizing —

utterly. ... Your music – well, I do not know how far above the tom-tom of the jungle it is, but it is not too far.

"These things you must watch. They all have their effects on the children. Make your home-life as near heaven-like as you can." (Relief Society Magazine, December 1952, p. 798.)

Holding Aloft of Standards

Youth leaders, are you holding aloft our standards or have you compromised them for the lowest common denominator in order to appease the deceived or vile within the Church? Are the dances and music in your cultural halls virtuous, lovely, praiseworthy, and of good report, or do they represent a modern Sodom with short skirts, loud beat, strobe lights, and darkness?

Will our youth leaders accept the standards set for young John Wesley by his mother? Hear her sound counsel:

"Would you judge of the lawfulness or unlawfulness of pleasure? Take this rule: Now note whatever weakens your reason, impairs the tenderness of your conscience, obscures your sense of God, takes off your relish for spiritual things, whatever increases the authority of the body over the mind, that thing is sin to you, however innocent it may seem in itself."

Have we, as Moroni warned, "polluted the holy church of God?" (Morm. 8:38.) The auxiliaries of the Church are to be a help, not a hindrance, to parents and the priesthood as they strive to lead their families back to God. Do any of us wear or display the broken cross, anti–Christ sign, that is the adversary's symbol of the so-called "peace movement"?

Lack of Knowledge

"My people are destroyed for lack of knowledge," lamented Hosea. (Hos. 4:6.) Today, because some parents have refused to become informed and then stand up and inform their children, they are witnessing the gradual physical and spiritual destruction of their posterity. If we would become like God, knowing good and evil, then we had best find out what is undermining us, how to avoid it, and what we can do about it.

It is time that the hearts of us fathers be turned to our children and the hearts of the children be turned to us fathers, or we shall both be cursed. The seeds of divorce are often sown and the blessings of children delayed by wives working outside the home. Working mothers should remember that their children usually need more of mother than of money.

Family Solidarity

As conditions in the world get progressively worse, it is crucial that the family draw closer together in righteousness and that family solidarity be established. As one has said, "There are too many pulls away from the home today. We should seriously consider whether or not too many activities and other interests take too much time and attention from our families, from our children, from those whom the Lord God gave us to love, to nourish, to teach, and to help through life."

> The stick-together families are happier by far
> Than the brothers and the sisters who take separate highways are.
> The gladdest people living are the wholesome folks who make
> A circle at the fireside that no power on earth can break.
> And the finest of conventions ever held beneath the sun
> Are the little family gatherings when the busy day is done.
> There are rich folk, there are poor folk, who imagine they are wise.
> And they're very quick to shatter all the little family ties.
> Each goes searching after pleasure in his own selected way.
> Each with strangers likes to wander and with strangers likes to play.
> But it's bitterness they harvest, and it's empty joy they find,
> For the children that are wisest are the stick-together kind.
> There are some who seem to fancy that for gladness they must roam,
> That for smiles that are the brightest they must wander far from home.
> That the strange friend is the true friend, and they travel far astray
> And they waste their lives in striving for a joy that's far away,
> But the gladdest sort of people, when the busy day is done,

Are the brothers and the sisters, who together share their fun.
It's the stick–together family that wins the joys of earth,
That hears the sweetest music and that finds the finest mirth;
It's the old home roof that shelters all the charm that life can give;
There you find the gladdest playground, there the happiest spot to live.
And, O weary, wandering brother, if contentment you would win,
Come you back unto the fireside and be comrade with your kin.
(Adapted from a poem by Edgar A. Guest.)

Strengthening the Family

And so let's strengthen the family. Family and individual prayer, morning and evening, can invite the blessings of the Lord on your household. Mealtime provides a wonderful time to review the activities of the day and to not only feed the body, but to feed the spirit as well with members of the family taking turns reading the scriptures, particularly, the Book of Mormon. Nighttime is a great time for the busy father to go to each child's bedside, to talk with him, answer his questions and tell him how much he is loved. In such homes there is no "generation gap." This deceptive phrase is another tool of the devil to weaken the home and family. Children who honor their parents and parents who love their children can make a home a haven of safety and a little bit of heaven.

Does this poem describe your family gatherings?

We are all here:
Father, mother,
Sister, brother,
All who hold each other dear.
Each chair is filled, we are all at home.
Tonight, let no cold stranger come;
It must be often thus around
Our old familiar hearth we're found.
Bless, then, the meeting and the spot,
For once be every care forgot;
Let gentle peace assert her power,

And kind affection rule the hour.
We're all–all here.
(Adapted from a poem by Charles Sprague.)

God bless us to strengthen our families by avoiding the crafty designs of the adversary and following the noble ways of the Lord, so that in due time we can report to our Heavenly Father in his celestial home that we are all there, father, mother, sister, brother, all who hold each other dear. Each chair is filled, we are all back home.
In the name, of Jesus Christ. Amen.

THE BOOK OF MORMON IS THE WORD OF GOD

I speak to you today on a most vital subject. As members of The Church of Jesus Christ of Latter-day Saints, "we believe ... the Book of Mormon to be the word of God." (A of F 1:8.) God has so declared it, so have its writers, so have its witnesses, and so do all those who have read it and received a personal revelation from God as to its truthfulness.

In section 20 of the Doctrine and Covenants the Lord says that he gave Joseph Smith "power from on high ... to translate the Book of Mormon; Which contains ... the fulness of the gospel of Jesus Christ ... ; Which was given by inspiration." (D&C 20:8–10.)

Nephi, one of the prophet-writers of the Book of Mormon, testifies that the book contains "the words of Christ" (2 Ne. 33:10), and Moroni, the last writer in the book, testifies that "these things are true." (Moro. 7:35.)

This same Moroni, as an angelic being sent from God, showed these ancient records to three witnesses in our day. Their testimony of the records is contained in the front the Book of Mormon. They state: "We also know that they have been translated by the gift and power of God, for his voice hath declared it unto us; wherefore we know of a surety that the work is true."

And Joseph Smith, the Prophet, the instrument whom God used to translate this record, testified that "the Book of Mormon was the most correct of any book on earth, and the keystone of our religion, and a man would get nearer to God by abiding by its precepts, than by any other book." (History of The Church of Jesus Christ of Latter-day Saints, 4:461.)

The Book of Mormon was written for us today. God is the author of the book. It is a record of a fallen people, compiled by inspired men for our blessing today. Those people never had the book—it was meant for us. Mormon, the ancient prophet after whom the book is named, abridged centuries of records. God, who knows the end from the beginning, told him what to include in his abridgment that we would need for our day. Mormon turned the records over to his son Moroni, the last recorder; and Moroni, writing over 1,500 years ago but speaking to us today, states: "Behold, I speak unto you as if ye were present, and yet ye are not. But behold, Jesus Christ hath shown you unto me, and I know your doing." (Morm. 8:35.)

The purpose of the Book of Mormon is stated on the title page. It is "to the convincing of the Jew and Gentile that Jesus is the Christ, the Eternal God."

Nephi, the first prophet-writer in the Book of Mormon, states: "For the fulness of mine intent is that I may persuade men to come unto the God of Abraham, and the God of Isaac, and the God of Jacob, and be saved.

"Wherefore, the things which are pleasing unto the world I do not write, but the things which are pleasing unto God and unto those who are not of the world.

"Wherefore, I shall give commandment unto my seed, that they shall not occupy these plates with things which are not of worth unto the children of men." (1 Ne. 6:4–6.)

The Book of Mormon brings men to Christ through two basic means. First, it tells in a plain manner of Christ and his gospel. It testifies of his divinity and of the necessity for a Redeemer and the need of our putting trust in him. It bears witness of the Fall and the Atonement and the first principles of the gospel, including our need of a broken heart and a contrite spirit and a spiritual rebirth. It proclaims we must endure to the end in righteousness and live the moral life of a Saint.

Second, the Book of Mormon exposes the enemies of Christ. It confounds false doctrines and lays down contention. (See 2 Ne. 3:12.) It fortifies the humble followers of Christ against the evil designs, strategies, and doctrines of the devil in our day. The type of apostates in the Book of Mormon are similar to the type we have today. God, with his infinite foreknowledge, so molded the Book of Mormon that we might see the error and know how to combat false educational, political, religious, and philosophical concepts of our time.

Now God expects us to use the Book of Mormon in several ways. We are to read it ourselves – carefully, prayerfully – and ponder as we read, as to whether this book is the work of God or of an unlearned youth. And then when we are finished reading the things in the book, Moroni exhorts us to put them to the test in these words:

"And when ye shall receive these things, I would exhort you that ye would ask God, the Eternal Father, in the name of Christ, if these things are not true; and if ye shall ask with a sincere heart, with real intent, having faith in Christ, he will manifest the truth of it unto you, by the power of the Holy Ghost." (Moro. 10:4.) I have done as Moroni exhorts, and I can testify to you that this book is from God and so is verily true.

We are to use the Book of Mormon as the basis for our teaching. In section 42 of the Doctrine and Covenants, the Lord states: "And again, the elders, priests and teachers of this church shall teach the principles of my gospel, which are in … the Book of Mormon, in the which is the fulness of the gospel." (D&C 42:12.)

As we read and teach, we are to liken the Book of Mormon scriptures unto us "that it might be for our profit and learning." (1 Ne. 19:23.)

We are to use the Book of Mormon in handling objections to the Church. God the Father and his Son Jesus Christ revealed themselves to Joseph Smith in a marvelous vision. After that glorious event, Joseph Smith told a minister about it. Joseph was surprised to hear the minister say that there were no such things as visions or revelations in these days, that all such things had ceased. (See JS–H 1:21.)

This remark symbolizes practically all of the objections that have ever been made against the Church by nonmembers and dissident members alike. Namely, they do not believe that God reveals his will today to the Church through prophets of God. All objections, whether they be on abortion, plural marriage, seventh-day worship, etc., basically hinge on whether Joseph Smith and his successors were and are prophets of God receiving divine revelation. Here, then, is a procedure to handle most objections through the use of the Book of Mormon.

— First, understand the objection.

— Second, give the answer from revelation.

— Third, show how the correctness of the answer really depends on whether or not we have modern revelation through modern prophets.

— Fourth, explain that whether or not we have modern prophets and revelation really depends on whether the Book of Mormon is true.

Therefore, the only problem the objector has to resolve for himself is whether the Book of Mormon is true. For if the Book of Mormon is true, then Jesus is the Christ, Joseph Smith was his prophet, The Church of Jesus Christ of Latter-day Saints is true, and it is being led today by a prophet receiving revelation.

Our main task is to declare the gospel and do it effectively. We are not obligated to answer every objection. Every man eventually is backed up to the wall of faith, and there he must make his stand. "And if they are not the words of Christ, judge ye," said Nephi, "for Christ will show unto you, with power and great glory, that they are his words, at the last day; and you and I shall stand face to face before his bar; and ye shall know that I have been commanded of him to write these things." (2 Ne. 33:11.) Every man must judge for himself, knowing God will hold him accountable.

The Book of Mormon is to be used "for a standard unto my people, which are of the house of Israel," the Lord says, and its words "shall hiss forth unto the ends of the earth." (2 Ne. 29:2.) We, the members of the Church, and particularly the missionaries, have to be the "hissers," or the tellers and testifiers, of the Book of Mormon unto the ends of the earth.

The Book of Mormon is the great standard we are to use. It shows that Joseph Smith was a prophet. It contains the words of Christ, and its great mission is to bring men to Christ and all other things are secondary. The golden question of the Book of Mormon is "Do you want to learn more of Christ?" The Book of Mormon is the great finder of the golden contact. It does not contain things which are "pleasing unto the world" (1 Ne. 6:5), and so the worldly are not interested in it. It is a great sieve.

Anyone who has diligently sought to know the doctrines and teachings of the Book of Mormon and has used it conscientiously in missionary work knows within his soul that this is the instrument which God has given to the missionaries to convince the Jew and Gentile and Lamanite of the truthfulness of our message.

Now, we have not been using the Book of Mormon as we should. Our homes are not as strong unless we are using it to bring our children to Christ. Our families may be corrupted by worldly trends and teachings unless we know how to use the book to expose and combat the falsehoods in socialism, organic evolution, rationalism, humanism, etc. Our missionaries are not as effective unless they are "hissing forth" with it. Social, ethical, cultural, or educational converts will not survive under the heat of the day unless their taproots go down to the fulness of the gospel which the Book of Mormon contains. Our Church classes are not as spirit-filled unless we hold it up as a standard. And our nation will continue to degenerate unless we read and heed the words of the God of this land, Jesus Christ, and quit building up and upholding the secret combinations which the Book of Mormon tells us proved the downfall of both previous American civilizations.

Some of the early missionaries, on returning home, were reproved by the Lord in section 84 of the Doctrine and Covenants because they had treated lightly the Book of Mormon. As a result, their minds had been darkened. The Lord said that this kind of treatment of the Book of Mormon brought the whole Church under condemnation, even all of the children of Zion. And then the Lord said, "And they shall remain under this condemnation until they repent and remember the new covenant, even the Book of Mormon." (See D&C 84:54–57.) Are we still under that condemnation?

Reading the Book of Mormon is one of the greatest persuaders to get men on missions. We need more missionaries. But we also need better-prepared missionaries coming out of the wards and branches and homes where they know and love the Book of Mormon. A great challenge and day of preparation is at hand for missionaries to meet and teach with the Book of Mormon. We need missionaries to match our message.

And now grave consequences hang on our response to the Book of Mormon. "Those who receive it," said the Lord, "in faith, and work righteousness, shall receive a crown of eternal life;

"But those who harden their hearts in unbelief, and reject it, it shall turn to their own condemnation–

"For the Lord God has spoken it." (D&C 20:14–16.)

Is the Book of Mormon true? Yes.

Who is it for? Us.

What is its purpose? To bring men to Christ.

How does it do this? By testifying of Christ and revealing his enemies.

How are we to use it? We are to get a testimony of it, we are to teach from it, we are to hold it up as a standard and "hiss it forth."

Have we been doing this? Not as we should, nor as we must.

Do eternal consequences rest upon our response to this book? Yes, either to our blessing or our condemnation.

Every Latter-day Saint should make the study of this book a lifetime pursuit. Otherwise he is placing his soul in jeopardy and neglecting that which could give spiritual and intellectual unity to his whole life. There is a difference between a convert who is built on the rock of Christ through the Book of Mormon and stays hold of that iron rod, and one who is not.

Over a quarter of a century ago I listened in this Tabernacle to these words: "A few years ago as I began to practice law, members of my family were a little uneasy. They were afraid I would lose my faith. I wanted to practice law, but I had an even greater desire to keep my testimony, and so I decided upon a little procedure which I recommend to you. For thirty minutes each morning before I began the day's work I read from the Book of Mormon . . . . and in just a few minutes a day I read the Book of Mormon through, every year, for nine years. I know that it kept me in harmony, so far as I did keep in harmony, with the Spirit of the Lord." (Conference Report, Apr. 1949, p. 36.) It will hold us as close to the Spirit of the Lord as anything I know. That was President Marion G. Romney. I echo his counsel.

What, then, are we to say of the Book of Mormon? I bear witness that it is verily true. I know this as I know that I live. We stand with the Prophet Joseph Smith when he said, "I told the brethren that the Book of Mormon was the most correct of any book on earth, and the keystone of our religion, and a man would get nearer to God by abiding by its precepts, than by any other book." (History of the Church, 4:461.)

May we know and use the keystone and get nearer to God, I pray in the name of Jesus Christ. Amen.

BEWARE OF PRIDE

My beloved brethren and sisters, I rejoice to be with you in another glorious general conference of the Church. How grateful I am for the love, prayers, and service of the devoted members of the Church throughout the world.

May I commend you faithful Saints who are striving to flood the earth and your lives with the Book of Mormon. Not only must we move forward in a monumental manner more copies of the Book of Mormon, but we must move boldly forward into our own lives and throughout the earth more of its marvelous messages.

This sacred volume was written for us – for our day. Its scriptures are to be likened unto ourselves. (See 1 Ne. 19:23.)

The Doctrine and Covenants tells us that the Book of Mormon is the "record of a fallen people." (D&C 20:9.) Why did they fall? This is one of the major messages of the Book of Mormon. Mormon gives the answer in the closing chapters of the book in these words: "Behold, the pride of this nation, or the people of the Nephites, hath proven their destruction." (Moro. 8:27.) And then, lest we miss that momentous Book of Mormon message from that fallen people, the Lord warns us in the Doctrine and Covenants, "Beware of pride, lest ye become as the Nephites of old." (D&C 38:39.)

I earnestly seek an interest in your faith and prayers as I strive to bring forth light on this Book of Mormon message – the sin of pride. This message has been weighing heavily on my soul for some time. I know the Lord wants this message delivered now.

In the pre-mortal council, it was pride that felled Lucifer, "a son of the morning." (2 Ne. 24:12–15; see also D&C 76:25–27; Moses 4:3.) At the end of this world, when God cleanses the earth by fire, the proud will be burned as stubble and the meek shall inherit the earth. (See 3 Ne. 12:5, 3 Ne. 25:1; D&C 29:9; JS–H 1:37; Mal. 4:1.)

Three times in the Doctrine and Covenants the Lord uses the phrase "beware of pride," including a warning to the second elder of the Church, Oliver Cowdery, and to Emma Smith, the wife of the Prophet. (D&C 23:1; see also D&C 25:14; D&C 38:39.)

Pride is a very misunderstood sin, and many are sinning in ignorance. (See Mosiah 3:11; 3 Ne. 6:18.) In the scriptures there is no such thing as righteous pride–it is always considered a sin. Therefore, no matter how the world uses the term, we must understand how God uses the term so we can understand the language of holy writ and profit thereby. (See 2 Ne. 4:15; Mosiah 1:3–7; Alma 5:61.)

Most of us think of pride as self-centeredness, conceit, boastfulness, arrogance, or haughtiness. All of these are elements of the sin, but the heart, or core, is still missing.

The central feature of pride is enmity – enmity toward God and enmity toward our fellowmen. Enmity means "hatred toward, hostility to, or a state of opposition." It is the power by which Satan wishes to reign over us.

Pride is essentially competitive in nature. We pit our will against God's. When we direct our pride toward God, it is in the spirit of "my will and not thine be done." As Paul said, they "seek their own, not the things which are Jesus Christ's." (Philip. 2:21.)

Our will in competition to God's will allows desires, appetites, and passions to go unbridled. (See Alma 38:12; 3 Ne. 12:30.)

The proud cannot accept the authority of God giving direction to their lives. (See Hel. 12:6.) They pit their perceptions of truth against

God's great knowledge, their abilities versus God's priesthood power, their accomplishments against His mighty works.

Our enmity toward God takes on many labels, such as rebellion, hard-heartedness, stiff-neckedness, unrepentant, puffed up, easily offended, and sign seekers. The proud wish God would agree with them. They aren't interested in changing their opinions to agree with God's.

Another major portion of this very prevalent sin of pride is enmity toward our fellowmen. We are tempted daily to elevate ourselves above others and diminish them. (See Hel. 6:17; D&C 58:41.)

The proud make every man their adversary by pitting their intellects, opinions, works, wealth, talents, or any other worldly measuring device against others. In the words of C. S. Lewis: "Pride gets no pleasure out of having something, only out of having more of it than the next man. … It is the comparison that makes you proud: the pleasure of being above the rest. Once the element of competition has gone, pride has gone." (Mere Christianity, New York: Macmillan, 1952, pp. 109–10.)

In the pre-earthly council, Lucifer placed his proposal in competition with the Father's plan as advocated by Jesus Christ. (See Moses 4:1–3.) He wished to be honored above all others. (See 2 Ne. 24:13.) In short, his prideful desire was to dethrone God. (See D&C 29:36; D&C 76:28.)

The scriptures abound with evidences of the severe consequences of the sin of pride to individuals, groups, cities, and nations. "Pride goeth before destruction." (Prov. 16:18.) It destroyed the Nephite nation and the city of Sodom. (See Moro. 8:27; Ezek. 16:49–50.)

It was through pride that Christ was crucified. The Pharisees were wroth because Jesus claimed to be the Son of God, which was a threat to their position, and so they plotted His death. (See John 11:53.)

Saul became an enemy to David through pride. He was jealous because the crowds of Israelite women were singing that "Saul hath slain his thousands, and David his ten thousands." (1 Sam. 18:6–8.)

The proud stand more in fear of men's judgment than of God's judgment. (See D&C 3:6–7; D&C 30:1–2; D&C 60:2.) "What will men think of me?" weighs heavier than "What will God think of me?"

King Noah was about to free the prophet Abinadi, but an appeal to his pride by his wicked priests sent Abinadi to the flames. (See Mosiah 17:11–12.) Herod sorrowed at the request of his wife to behead John the Baptist. But his prideful desire to look good to "them which sat with him at meat" caused him to kill John. (Matt. 14:9; see also Mark 6:26.)

Fear of men's judgment manifests itself in competition for men's approval. The proud love "the praise of men more than the praise of God." (John 12:42–43.) Our motives for the things we do are where the sin is manifest. Jesus said He did "always those things" that pleased God. (John 8:29.) Would we not do well to have the pleasing of God as our motive rather than to try to elevate ourselves above our brother and outdo another?

Some prideful people are not so concerned as to whether their wages meet their needs as they are that their wages are more than someone else's. Their reward is being a cut above the rest. This is the enmity of pride.

When pride has a hold on our hearts, we lose our independence of the world and deliver our freedoms to the bondage of men's judgment. The world shouts louder than the whisperings of the Holy Ghost. The reasoning of men overrides the revelations of God, and the proud let go of the iron rod. (See 1 Ne. 8:19–28; 1 Ne. 11:25; 1 Ne. 15:23–24.)

Pride is a sin that can readily be seen in others but is rarely admitted in ourselves. Most of us consider pride to be a sin of those on the top, such as the rich and the learned, looking down at the rest of us. (See 2 Ne. 9:42.) There is, however, a far more common ailment among us – and that is pride from the bottom looking up. It is manifest in so many ways, such as faultfinding, gossiping, backbiting, murmuring, living beyond our means, envying, coveting, withholding gratitude and praise that might lift another, and being unforgiving and jealous.

Disobedience is essentially a prideful power struggle against someone in authority over us. It can be a parent, a priesthood leader, a teacher, or ultimately God. A proud person hates the fact that someone is above him. He thinks this lowers his position.

Selfishness is one of the more common faces of pride. "How everything affects me" is the center of all that matters – self-conceit, self-pity, worldly self-fulfillment, self-gratification, and self-seeking.

Pride results in secret combinations which are built up to get power, gain, and glory of the world. (See Hel. 7:5; Ether 8:9, 16, 22–23; Moses 5:31.) This fruit of the sin of pride, namely secret combinations, brought down both the Jaredite and the Nephite civilizations and has been and will yet be the cause of the fall of many nations. (See Ether 8:18–25.)

Another face of pride is contention. Arguments, fights, unrighteous dominion, generation gaps, divorces, spouse abuse, riots, and disturbances all fall into this category of pride.

Contention in our families drives the Spirit of the Lord away. It also drives many of our family members away. Contention ranges from a hostile spoken word to worldwide conflicts. The scriptures tell us that "only by pride cometh contention." (Prov. 13:10; see also Prov. 28:25.)

The scriptures testify that the proud are easily offended and hold grudges. (See 1 Ne. 16:1–3.) They withhold forgiveness to keep another in their debt and to justify their injured feelings.

The proud do not receive counsel or correction easily. (See Prov. 15:10; Amos 5:10.) Defensiveness is used by them to justify and rationalize their frailties and failures. (See Matt. 3:9; John 6:30–59.)

The proud depend upon the world to tell them whether they have value or not. Their self–esteem is determined by where they are judged to be on the ladders of worldly success. They feel worthwhile as individuals if the numbers beneath them in achievement, talent, beauty, or intellect are large enough. Pride is ugly. It says, "If you succeed, I am a failure."

If we love God, do His will, and fear His judgment more than men's, we will have self-esteem.

Pride is a damning sin in the true sense of that word. It limits or stops progression. (See Alma 12:10–11.) The proud are not easily taught. (See 1 Ne. 15:3, 7–11.) They won't change their minds to accept truths, because to do so implies they have been wrong.

Pride adversely affects all our relationships – our relationship with God and His servants, between husband and wife, parent and child, employer and employee, teacher and student, and all mankind. Our degree of pride determines how we treat our God and our brothers and sisters. Christ wants to lift us to where He is. Do we desire to do the same for others?

Pride fades our feelings of sonship to God and brotherhood to man. It separates and divides us by "ranks," according to our "riches" and our "chances for learning." (3 Ne. 6:12.) Unity is impossible for a proud people, and unless we are one we are not the Lord's. (See Mosiah 18:21; D&C 38:27; D&C 105:2–4; Moses 7:18.)

Think of what pride has cost us in the past and what it is now costing us in our own lives, our families, and the Church.

Think of the repentance that could take place with lives changed, marriages preserved, and homes strengthened, if pride did not keep us from confessing our sins and forsaking them. (See D&C 58:43.)

Think of the many who are less active members of the Church because they were offended and their pride will not allow them to forgive or fully sup at the Lord's table.

Think of the tens of thousands of additional young men and couples who could be on missions except for the pride that keeps them from yielding their hearts unto God. (See Alma 10:6; Hel. 3:34–35.)

Think how temple work would increase if the time spent in this godly service were more important than the many prideful pursuits that compete for our time.

Pride affects all of us at various times and in various degrees. Now you can see why the building in Lehi's dream that represents the pride of the world was large and spacious and great was the multitude that did enter into it. (See 1 Ne. 8:26, 33; 1 Ne. 11:35–36.)

Pride is the universal sin, the great vice. Yes, pride is the universal sin, the great vice.

The antidote for pride is humility – meekness, submissiveness. (See Alma 7:23.) It is the broken heart and contrite spirit. (See 3 Ne. 9:20; 3 Ne. 12:19; D&C 20:37; D&C 59:8; Ps. 34:18; Isa. 57:15; Isa. 66:2.) As Rudyard Kipling put it so well:

The tumult and the shouting dies;
The captains and the kings depart.
Still stands thine ancient sacrifice,
An humble and a contrite heart.
Lord God of Hosts, be with us yet,
Lest we forget, lest we forget.
(Hymns, 1985, no. 80.)

God will have a humble people. Either we can choose to be humble or we can be compelled to be humble. Alma said, "Blessed are they who humble themselves without being compelled to be humble." (Alma 32:16.)

Let us choose to be humble.

We can choose to humble ourselves by conquering enmity toward our brothers and sisters, esteeming them as ourselves, and lifting them as high or higher than we are. (See D&C 38:24; D&C 81:5; D&C 84:106.)

We can choose to humble ourselves by receiving counsel and chastisement. (See Jacob 4:10; Hel. 15:3; D&C 63:55; D&C 101:4–5; D&C 108:1; D&C 124:61, 84; D&C 136:31; Prov. 9:8.)

We can choose to humble ourselves by forgiving those who have offended us. (See 3 Ne. 13:11, 14; D&C 64:10.)

We can choose to humble ourselves by rendering selfless service. (See Mosiah 2:16–17.)

We can choose to humble ourselves by going on missions and preaching the word that can humble others. (See Alma 4:19; Alma 31:5; Alma 48:20.)

We can choose to humble ourselves by getting to the temple more frequently.

We can choose to humble ourselves by confessing and forsaking our sins and being born of God. (See D&C 58:43; Mosiah 27:25–26; Alma 5:7–14, 49.)

We can choose to humble ourselves by loving God, submitting our will to His, and putting Him first in our lives. (See 3 Ne. 11:11; 3 Ne. 13:33; Moro. 10:32.)

Let us choose to be humble. We can do it. I know we can.

My dear brethren and sisters, we must prepare to redeem Zion. It was essentially the sin of pride that kept us from establishing Zion in the days of the Prophet Joseph Smith. It was the same sin of pride that brought consecration to an end among the Nephites. (See 4 Ne. 1:24–25.)

Pride is the great stumbling block to Zion. I repeat: Pride is the great stumbling block to Zion.

We must cleanse the inner vessel by conquering pride. (See Alma 6:2–4; Matt. 23:25–26.)

We must yield "to the enticings of the Holy Spirit," put off the prideful "natural man," become "a saint through the atonement of Christ the Lord," and become "as a child, submissive, meek, humble." (Mosiah 3:19; see also Alma 13:28.)

That we may do so and go on to fulfill our divine destiny is my fervent prayer in the name of Jesus Christ, amen.

THE TWELFTH ARTICLE OF FAITH

When the Prophet Joseph Smith outlined the Articles of Faith, he set forth in clear, unmistakable terms the foundations of our worship and of our relationships with one another. In view of the troubled times which the nations of the earth are experiencing at present, it is well for us as members of the Lord's kingdom to understand clearly our responsibilities and obligations respecting governments and laws as declared in the Twelfth Article of Faith: "We believe in being subject to kings, presidents, rulers, and magistrates, in obeying, honoring, and sustaining the law."

In it is a declaration requiring obedience, loyalty to, and respect for duly constituted laws and the officials administering those laws. In justifying such loyal compliance, however, the Lord also promulgated certain safeguards and conditions which must be observed if freedom and liberty are to be preserved and enjoyed. These are emphasized primarily in the 98th and 134th sections of the Doctrine and Covenants. How I wish these fundamental concepts were emblazoned on the hearts of all our people!

It seems to me there are two thoughts with regard to governments and laws which might profitably be considered at this time. One relates to the people who administer the laws and the other to the laws themselves. Concerning our public officials, the Lord has counseled:

"Nevertheless, when the wicked rule the people mourn. Wherefore, honest men and wise men should be sought for diligently, and good men and wise men ye should observe to uphold; otherwise whatsoever is less than these cometh of evil." (D&C 98:9–10.)

These admonitions, in my humble judgment, are just as binding upon the Latter-day Saints as are the law of tithing, the Word of Wisdom, and baptism. We should seek out honest men and wise men to hold political office in our respective governments. This is the will of the Lord as spoken by revelation.

Many people have had cause for serious reflection of late as they have observed the rise and fall of once glorious and powerful nations. Why, they ask, have nations which have contributed so richly to the fields of literature, music, and the arts and sciences permitted selfish, ambitious men to rise to great power as has been evidenced in several European nations? One of the important reasons, as I have observed it firsthand, is the fact that the citizens generally failed to carry out the admonition which the Lord has given the Latter-day Saints: to seek out their good and wise men to serve as their leaders in political capacities. Men without faith in eternal principles were permitted to rise to power.

We must not think it cannot happen here. We must be eternally vigilant as Latter-day Saints and inspire in the lives of our children a love for eternal principles and a desire to seek out honorable men – the best possible – to stand at the head of our political governments, local, state, and federal. Only in this way can we safeguard the liberties which have been vouchsafed to us as our inalienable rights. Unless we do so, we may very easily lose them because of our indifference, because of our failure to exercise our franchise, because we permit men who are unworthy to rise to positions of political power.

Not only should we seek humble, worthy, courageous leadership; but we should also measure all proposals having to do with our national or local welfare by four standards:

First, is the proposal, the policy, or the idea being promoted right as measured by the gospel of Jesus Christ? I assure you it is much easier for one to measure a proposed policy by the gospel of Jesus Christ if he has accepted the gospel and is living it.

Second, is it right as measured by the Lord's standard of constitutional government, wherein he says: "And that law of the land which is constitutional, supporting that principle of freedom in maintaining rights and privileges, belongs to all mankind, and is justifiable before me"? (D&C 98:5.) Whether we live under a divinely inspired constitution, as in the United States, or under some other form of government, the Lord's standard is a safe guide.

Third, we might well ask, is it right as measured by the counsel of the living oracles of God? It is my conviction that these living oracles are not only authorized, but are also obligated to give counsel to this people on any subject that is vital to the welfare of this people and to the up-building of the kingdom of God. So that measure should be applied.

Fourth, what will be the effect upon the morale and the character of the people if this or that policy is adopted? After all, as a church, we are interested in building men and women and in building character, because character is the one thing we make in this world and take with us into the next. It must never be sacrificed for expediency.

May we do our duty as citizens and as members of the Church to see to it that the right kind of people are elected to public office, so that the rich blessings that we now enjoy and that have been promised to us may be realized in all the days to come. May we likewise use wisdom and care as we evaluate various proposals and programs, so men everywhere may come to know the joy of living under wise laws honorably administered by men and women intent upon preserving and strengthening man's free agency and ennobling his character.

THE CONSTITUTION: A HEAVENLY BANNER

On the seventeenth day of September 1987, we, commemorate the two-hundredth birthday of the Constitutional Convention, which gave birth to the document that Gladstone said is "the most wonderful work ever struck off at a given time by the brain and purpose of man" (William Ewart Gladstone: Life and Public Services, ed. Thomas W. Handford [Chicago: The Dominion Co., 1899], p. 323).

I heartily endorse this assessment, and today I would like to pay honor – honor to the document itself, honor to the men who framed it, and honor to the God who inspired it and made possible its coming forth.

Some Basic Principles

To understand the significance of the Constitution, we must first understand some basic, eternal principles. These principles have their beginning in the premortal councils of heaven.

The Principle of Agency

The first basic principle is agency. The central issue in the premortal council was: Shall the children of God have untrammeled agency to choose the course they should follow, whether good or evil, or shall they be coerced and forced to be obedient? Christ and all who followed him stood for the former proposition – freedom of choice; Satan stood for the latter – coercion and force. The war that began in heaven over this issue is not yet over. The conflict continues on the battlefield of mortality. And one of Lucifer's primary strategies has been to restrict our agency through the power of earthly governments.

Look back in retrospect on almost six thousand years of human history! Freedom's moments have been infrequent and exceptional. We must appreciate that we live in one of history's most exceptional moments – in a nation and a time of unprecedented freedom. Freedom as we know it has been experienced by perhaps less than one percent of the human family.

The Proper Role of Government

The second basic principle concerns the function and proper role of government. These are the principles that, in my opinion, proclaim the proper role of government in the domestic affairs of the nation.

[I] believe that governments were instituted of God for the benefit of man; and that he holds men accountable for their acts in relation to them....

[I] believe that no government can exist in peace, except such laws are framed and held inviolate as will secure to each individual the free exercise of conscience, the right and control of property, and the protection of life....

[I] believe that all men are bound to sustain and uphold the respective governments in which they reside, while protected in their inherent and inalienable rights by the laws of such governments. [D&C 134:1–2, 5]

In other words, the most important single function of government is to secure the rights and freedoms of individual citizens.

The Source of Human Rights

The third important principle pertains to the source of basic human rights. Rights are either God-given as part of the divine plan, or they are granted by government as part of the political plan. If we accept the premise that human rights are granted by government, then we must be willing to accept the corollary that they can be denied by government. I, for one, shall never accept that premise. We must ever keep in mind the inspired words of Thomas Jefferson, as found in the Declaration of Independence:

We hold these truths to be self-evident, that all men are created equal, that they are endowed by their Creator with certain unalienable Rights, that among these are Life, Liberty, and the pursuit of Happiness. That to secure these rights, Governments are instituted among Men, deriving their just powers from the consent of the governed.

People Are Superior to Governments

The fourth basic principle we must understand is that people are superior to the governments they form. Since God created people with certain inalienable rights, and they, in turn, created government to help secure and safeguard those rights, it follows that the people are superior to the creature they created.

Governments Should Have Limited Powers

The fifth and final principle that is basic to our understanding of the Constitution is that governments should have only limited powers. The important thing to keep in mind is that the people who have created their government can give to that government only such powers as they, themselves, have in the first place. Obviously, they cannot give that which they do not possess. By deriving its just powers from the governed, government becomes primarily a mechanism for defense against bodily harm, theft, and involuntary servitude. It cannot claim the power to redistribute money or property nor to force reluctant citizens to perform acts of charity against their will. Government is created by the people. No individual possesses the power to take another's wealth or to force others to do good, so no government has the right to do such things either. The creature cannot exceed the creator.

The Constitution and Its Coming Forth

With these basic principles firmly in mind, let us now turn to a discussion of the inspired document we call the Constitution. My purpose is not to recite the events that led to the American Revolution

—we are all familiar with these. But I would say this: History is not an accident. Events are foreknown to God. His superintending influence is behind the actions of his righteous children. Long before America was even discovered, the Lord was moving and shaping events that would lead to the coming forth of the remarkable form of government established by the Constitution. America had to be free and independent to fulfill this destiny. I commend to you as excellent reading on this subject Elder Mark E. Petersen's book The Great Prologue (Salt Lake City: Deseret Book Co., 1975). As expressed so eloquently by John Adams before the signing of the Declaration, "There's a Divinity which shapes our ends" (quoted in The Works of Daniel Webster, vol. 1 (Boston: Charles C. Little and James Brown, 1851), p. 133). Though mortal eyes and minds cannot fathom the end from the beginning, God does.

God Raised Up Wise Men to Create the Constitution

In a revelation to the Prophet Joseph Smith, the Savior declared, "I established the Constitution of this land, by the hands of wise men whom I raised up unto this very purpose" (D&C 101:80). These were not ordinary men, but men chosen and held in reserve by the Lord for this very purpose.

Shortly after President Kimball became President of the Church, he assigned me to go into the vault of the St. George Temple and check the early records. As I did so, I realized the fulfillment of a dream I had had ever since learning of the visit of the Founding Fathers to the St. George Temple. I saw with my own eyes the records of the work that was done for the Founding Fathers of this great nation, beginning with George Washington. Think of it, the Founding Fathers of this nation, those great men, appeared within those sacred walls and had their vicarious work done for them. President Wilford Woodruff spoke of it in these words:

"Before I left St. George, the spirits of the dead gathered around me, wanting to know why we did not redeem them. Said they, 'You have had the use of the Endowment House for a number of years, and yet nothing has ever been done for us. We laid the foundation of the government you now enjoy, and we never apostatized from it, but we remained true to it and were faithful to God." These were the signers of the Declaration of Independence, and they waited on me for two days and two nights....

"I straightway went into the baptismal font and called upon Brother McCallister to baptize me for the signers of the Declaration of Independence, and fifty other eminent men. [Discourses of Wilford Woodruff, sel. G. Homer Durham (Salt Lake City: Bookcraft, 1946), pp. 160–61]

"These noble spirits came there with divine permission – evidence that this work of salvation goes forward on both sides of the veil."

At a later conference, in April 1898, after he became President of the Church, President Woodruff declared that "those men who laid the foundation of this American government and signed the Declaration of Independence were the best spirits the God of heaven could find on the face of the earth. They were choice spirits ... [and] were inspired of the Lord" (CR, April 1898, p. 89). We honor those men today. We are the grateful beneficiaries of their noble work.

The Lord Approved The Constitution

But we honor more than those who brought forth the Constitution. We honor the Lord who revealed it. God himself has borne witness to the fact that he is pleased with the final product of the work of these great patriots.

In a revelation to the Prophet Joseph Smith on August 6, 1833, the Savior admonished: "I, the Lord, justify you, and your brethren of my church, in befriending that law which is the constitutional law of the land" (D&C 98:6).

In the Kirtland Temple dedicatory prayer, given on March 27, 1836, the Lord directed the Prophet Joseph to say: "May those principles, which were so honorably and nobly defended, namely, the Constitution of our land, by our fathers, be established forever" (D&C 109:54).

A few years later, Joseph Smith, while unjustly incarcerated in a cold and depressing cell of Liberty Jail at Clay County, Missouri, frequently bore his testimony of the document's divinity: "The Constitution of the United States is a glorious standard; it is founded in the wisdom of God. It is a heavenly banner" (HC 3:304).

How this document accomplished all of this merits our further consideration.

The Document Itself

The Constitution consists of seven separate articles. The first three establish the three branches of our government: the legislative, the executive, and the judicial. The fourth article describes matters pertaining to states, most significantly the guarantee of a republican form of government to every state of the Union. Article 5 defines the amendment procedure of the document, a deliberately difficult process that should be clearly understood by every citizen. Article 6 covers several miscellaneous items, including a definition of the supreme law of the land, namely, the Constitution itself. Article 7, the last, explains how the Constitution is to be ratified. After ratification of the document, ten amendments were added and designated as our Bill of Rights.

Now to look at some of the major provisions of the document itself. Many principles could be examined, but I mention five as being crucial to the preservation of our freedom. If we understand the workability of these, we have taken the first step in defending our freedoms.

Major Provisions of the Document

The major provisions of the Constitution are as follows.

Sovereignty of the People

First: Sovereignty lies in the people themselves. Every governmental system has a sovereign, one or several who possess all the executive, legislative, and judicial powers. That sovereign may be an individual, a group, or the people themselves. The Founding Fathers believed in common law, which holds that true sovereignty rests with the people. Believing this to be in accord with truth, they inserted this imperative in the Declaration of Independence: "To secure these rights [life, liberty, and the pursuit of happiness], Governments are instituted among Men, deriving their just powers from the consent of the governed."

Separation of Powers

Second: To safeguard these rights, the Founding Fathers provided for the separation of powers among the three branches of government – the legislative, the executive, and the judicial. Each was to be independent of the other, yet each was to work in a unified relationship. As the great constitutionalist President J. Reuben Clark noted:

It is [the] union of independence and dependence of these branches – legislative, executive and judicial – and of the governmental functions possessed by each of them, that constitutes the marvelous genius of this unrivalled document.... It was here that the divine inspiration came. It was truly a miracle. [Church News, November 29, 1952, p. 12]

The use of checks and balances was deliberately designed, first, to make it difficult for a minority of the people to control the government, and, second, to place restraint on the government itself.

Limited Powers of Government

Third: The powers the people granted to the three branches of government were specifically limited. The Founding Fathers well understood human nature and its tendency to exercise unrighteous dominion when given authority. A constitution was therefore designed to limit government to certain enumerated functions, beyond which was tyranny.

The Principle of Representation

Fourth: Our constitutional government is based on the principle of representation. The principle of representation means that we have delegated to an elected official the power to represent us. The Constitution provides for both direct representation and indirect representation. Both forms of representation provide a tempering influence on pure democracy. The intent was to protect the individual's and the minority's rights to life, liberty, and the fruits of their labors– property. These rights were not to be subject to majority vote.

A Moral and Righteous People

Fifth: The Constitution was designed to work with only a moral and righteous people. "Our constitution," said John Adams (first vice-president and second president of the United States), "was made only for a moral and religious people. It is wholly inadequate to the government of any other" (John R. Howe, Jr., The Changing Political Thought of John Adams, Princeton University Press, 1966, p. 185).

The Crisis of Our Constitution

This, then, is the ingenious and inspired document created by these good and wise men for the benefit and blessing of future generations. It is now two hundred years since the Constitution was written. Have we been wise beneficiaries of the gift entrusted to us? Have we valued and protected the principles laid down by this great document?

At this bicentennial celebration we must, with sadness, say that we have not been wise in keeping the trust of our Founding Fathers. For the past two centuries, those who do not prize freedom have chipped away at every major clause of our Constitution until today we face a crisis of great dimensions.

The Prophecy of Joseph Smith

We are fast approaching that moment prophesied by Joseph Smith when he said:

"Even this Nation will be on the very verge of crumbling to pieces and tumbling to the ground and when the constitution is upon the brink of ruin this people will be the Staff upon which the Nation shall lean and they shall bear the constitution away from the very verge of destruction." [In Howard and Martha Coray Notebook, July 19, 1840, quoted by Andrew F. Eliat and Lyndon W. Cook, comps. and eds., TheWords of Joseph Smith (Provo, Utah: Religious Studies Center, Brigham Young University, 1980), p. 416]

The Need to Prepare

Will we be prepared? Will we be among those who will "bear the Constitution away from the very verge of destruction"? If we desire to be numbered among those who will, here are some things we must do:

1. We must be righteous and moral. We must live the gospel principles—all of them. We have no right to expect a higher degree of morality from those who represent us than what we ourselves are. To live a higher law means we will not seek to receive what we have not earned by our own labor. It means we will remember that government owes us nothing. It means we will keep the laws of the land. It means we will look to God as our Lawgiver and the source of our liberty.

2. We must learn the principles of the Constitution and then abide by its precepts. Have we read the Constitution and pondered it? Are we aware of its principles? Could we defend it? Can we recognize when a law is constitutionally unsound? The Church will not tell us how to do this, but we are admonished to do it. I quote Abraham Lincoln:

Let [the Constitution] be taught in schools, in seminaries, and in colleges; let it be written in primers, spelling–books, and in almanacs; let it be preached from the pulpit, proclaimed in legislative halls, and enforced in courts of justice. And, in short, let it become the political religion of the nation. [Complete Works of Abraham Lincoln, ed. John G. Nicolay and John Hay, vol. I (New York: Francis D. Tandy Co., 1905), p. 43]

3. We must become involved in civic affairs. As citizens of this republic, we cannot do our duty and be idle spectators. It is vital that we follow this counsel from the Lord: "Honest men and wise men should be sought for diligently, and good men and wise men ye should observe to uphold; otherwise whatsoever is less than these cometh of evil" (D&C 98:10). Note the qualities that the Lord demands in those who are to represent us. They must be good, wise, and honest. We must be concerted in our desires and efforts to see men and women represent us who possess all three of these qualities.

4. We must make our influence felt by our vote, our letters, and our advice. We must be wisely informed and let others know how we feel. We must take part in local precinct meetings and select delegates who will truly represent our feelings.

I have faith that the Constitution will be saved as prophesied by Joseph Smith. But it will not be saved in Washington. It will be saved by the citizens of this nation who love and cherish freedom. It will be saved by enlightened members of this Church – men and women who will subscribe to and abide by the principles of the Constitution.

The Constitution Requires Our Loyalty and Support

I reverence the Constitution of the United States as a sacred document. To me its words are akin to the revelations of God, for God has placed his stamp of approval on the Constitution of this land. I testify that the God of heaven sent some of his choicest spirits to lay the foundation of this government, and he has sent other choice spirits – even you who hear my words this day – to preserve it.

We, the blessed beneficiaries, face difficult days in this beloved land, "a land which is choice above all other lands" (Ether 2:10). It may also cost us blood before we are through. It is my conviction, however, that when the Lord comes, the Stars and Stripes will be floating on the breeze over this people. May it be so, and may God give us the faith and the courage exhibited by those patriots who pledged their lives and fortunes that we might be free, in the name of Jesus Christ. Amen.

STAND UP FOR FREEDOM

Humbly and gratefully I stand before you – grateful for patriots such as you – humbled by the magnitude of the task before us.

I speak to you as a fellow citizen of the United States of America deeply concerned about the welfare of our beloved country.

I am not here to tickle your ears – to entertain you. I will talk to you frankly and honestly. The message I bring is not a happy one, but it is the truth, and time is always on the side of truth. As the German philosopher Goethe, said: "Truth must be repeated again and again because error is constantly being preached round about."

I realize that the bearer of bad news is always unpopular. As a people we love sweetness and light – especially sweetness. Ralph Waldo Emerson said that every mind must make a choice between truth and repose. Those who will learn nothing from history are condemned to repeat it. This we are doing in the Americas today.

George Washington stated, "Truth will ultimately prevail where there are pains taken to bring it to light." To bring the truth to light is our challenge – this day and everyday.

"And ye shall know the truth, and the truth shall make you free." (John 8:32)

Returning recently from two years abroad has caused me to reflect seriously on recent trends and present conditions in our beloved country. I am shocked and saddened at what I find. I am sorry to say that all is not well in so-called prosperous, wealthy and powerful America.

We have moved a long way – and are now moving further and more rapidly down the soul–destroying road of socialism. The evidence is clear – shockingly clear for all to see.

With our national prestige at – or near – an embarrassing all-time low, we continue to weaken our domestic economy by unsound fiscal, economic and foreign aid policies which corrupt our national currency. Ever increasing centralization of power in the federal government in Washington, D.C. is reducing our local and state governments to virtual federal field offices while weakening individual initiative, enterprise and character.

With the crass unconstitutional usurpation of powers by the Executive Branch of the federal government, anti–spiritual decisions of the Supreme Court – all apparently approved by a weakly submissive rubber–stamp congress – the days ahead are ominously frightening.

Surely – certainly – it behooves patriotic citizens – such as you – to meet together to seriously consider present conditions in our beloved nation. It is imperative that American citizens become alerted and informed regarding the threat to our welfare, happiness and freedom.

No American is worthy of citizenship in this great land who refuses to take an active interest in these important matters.

All we hold dear as a great Christian nation is at stake.

A recent development has been the call for national unity. I believe there needs to be a unity in our land. But it must not be blind, senseless, irresponsible unity. It should not be a unity just for the sake of unity. It needs to be a unity built on sound principles.

We Americans have strayed far from sound principles – morally, Constitutionally and historically. It has been getting us into a quagmire of trouble all over the world, and especially here at home.

Americans at the grass roots level have sensed that their way of life is being threatened. During the last several years there has been a rising tide of resistance to the prevailing political trend. Compromises with Communism abroad and flirtations with socialism at home have stirred up opposition in both political parties. If this has lead to disunity then by all means let us return to a program of sound Constitutional principles on which we can unite.

There would be no virtue in calling for unity to support certain legislation if the majority of Americans were opposed to it. And the fact that both Democrats and Republicans in congress have at times resisted certain legislation shows that the Executive branch of the government may get out of step with the people.

I believe the American people know what they want. It would appear that the people want their civil rights safeguarded but not a destruction of states' rights.

The farmers want opportunity for reasonable income security but not agricultural "dictatorship" security.

Parents want better school for their children but not a federal subsidy leading to control of the teachings and text books as well as the ideologies of the children.

People want sound pay-as-you go spending with a balanced budget, not reckless spending and tax cuts with an unbalanced budget.

If there is a need for urban renewal, people want it under local direction, not under the red tape of Washington bureaus armed with confiscatory powers over property.

People want the development of power dams but not the strangulation of privately – owned power companies which have proven far more efficient and economical than utilities run by the government.

In other words, there are some legitimate functions and services which the Federal Government can and should provide, but those who want the federal power to exceed the authority delegated to it by the Constitution will be resisted both by Democrats and Republicans. This is what is happening in some limited areas today, may the trend increase.

And anyone who tries to equate this love of Constitutional principles as meaning hatred of our national leaders is using Goebbels-style deception. History has already demonstrated that conservative opposition to national leaders was not "hate" but an attempt to do them a favor.

Let me give you some examples:

Was it "hate" when General Albert C. Whedemeyer pleaded with general Marshal and President Truman to reverse their policy before they lost china?

Was it "hate" when Whitaker Chambers tried to warn President Roosevelt in 1939 that Alger Hiss had been giving the Soviet Union more espionage data than any other member of the Washington spy network?

Was it "hate" when J. Edgar Hoover tried to warn President Truman that Harry Dexter White was a member of the Soviet spy apparatus and was doing great danger to the nation as Assistant-Secretary of the Treasury?

Was it "hate" when I went to the Secretary of State under President Eisenhower and pleaded with him not to support the Communist, Fidel Castro?

Was it "hate" when I urged the President of the United States to go to the aid of the brave freedom fighters in Hungary?

Was it "hate" when the Democratic Senator from Connecticut, Thomas Dodd, pleaded for two years with the President not to support the United Nations blood bath against the free people of Katanga?

Is it "hate" when distinguished military leaders advise that an all out effort could end the Viet Nam struggle almost over night?

This list of acts by well-meaning citizens who want and wanted to prevent their Presidents from making serious mistakes could be extended at length. But they would all illustrate the same point. History will show that many terrible mistakes occurred because the advice of these well informed and well–meaning citizens was not heeded.

Therefore, I repeat, this kind of resistance to a national leader is rooted in love and respect, not hate. Regardless of which political party is in power, you do not want to see your President make a serious blunder. You don't want him to lose China. You don't want him to allow the enemy agents to make fools of us. You don't want him to lose Cuba. You don't want him to suffer the humiliation of a "Bay of Pigs disaster", or allow a Soviet Gibraltar to be built 90 miles from our shores.

Every one of these events which have been so disastrous and which have destroyed freedom for hundreds of millions of our allies, could have been prevented. And the voices of those who tried to warn Washington of what was coming cannot be attributed to hate. It has been out of a love for our country and respect for our leaders that the voice of warning has been raised.

What causes one to wonder is why these warnings were not carefully considered and acted upon. Why is it that men in high places in government, regardless of party have been deceived? I am convinced that a major part of the cause can be justly laid at the door of the Socialist-Communist Conspiracy, which is lead by masters of deceit who deceive the very elect. J. Edgar Hoover put it well when he said, "I would have no fears if more Americans possessed the zeal, the fervor, the persistence, and the industry to learn about this menace of Red fascism. I do fear for the liberal and progressive who have been hoodwinked and duped into joining with the Communists."

Therefore, let those who call for unity and the elimination of hate be sure they are not merely trying to silence the friends of freedom. These are they who respect their leaders and resist them only when it is felt they are headed for a catastrophe. What patriotic American would wish to stand silent if he saw the President verging on a blunder because of bad advice or a mistake in judgment of the facts?

I believe one of the most serious mistakes a President could make would be to weaken the Constitution.

From the time I was a small boy, I was taught that the American Constitution is an inspired document. I was also taught that the day will come when the Constitution will be endangered and hang as it were by a single thread. I was taught that we should study the Constitution, preserve its principles and defend it against any who would destroy it. To the best of my ability I have always tried to do this. I expect to continue my efforts to help protect and safeguard our inspired Constitution.

Some two years ago, however, a critic from Washington, D.C. claimed that a person who serves in a church capacity should not comment on such matters. He charged that the separation of church and state requires that church officials restrict their attention to affairs of the Church.

I, of course, also believe that the institutions of church and state should be separated, but I also do not agree that spiritual leaders cannot comment on basic issues which involve the very foundation of American liberty.

In fact, if this were true, we would have to throw away a substantial part of the Bible. Speaking out against immoral or unjust actions of political leaders has been the burden of prophets and disciples of God from time immemorial. It was for this very reason that many of them were persecuted. Some of them were stoned, some of them were burned, many were imprisoned. Nevertheless it was their God-given task, as watchmen on the towers, to speak up.

It is certainly no different today.

To Moses God said: "....proclaim liberty throughout all the land unto all the inhabitants thereof." (Lev. 25:10)

Why? For God knows full well that the gospel – His plan for the blessing of His children can prosper only in an atmosphere of freedom.

To modern men God has said: the Constitution "should be maintained for the rights and protection of all flesh." (Doctrine and Covenants 101:77)

Is the Constitution being maintained or is it in jeopardy? Senator J. William Fulbright of Arkansas, says the American Constitution is nothing more than a product of the Eighteenth Century agrarian society. It is now obsolete he claims. Senator Joseph S. Park of Pennsylvania says the separation of powers with its checks and balances must be curtailed because they keep the President from making quick and decisive decisions. Gus Hall, head of the Communist Party U.S.A., agrees with these two Senators – yes – Gus Hall agrees with these two senators and demands that there should be a new federal charter eliminating states' rights. America's national sovereignty should be abandoned according to Walt Rostow, chairman of the State Department Policy Planning Board. He has boldly demanded "an end of nationhood as it has been historically defined." (Quoted in the extension of remarks by Senator Strom Thurmond, Congressional Record, June 6, 1963, pp. A3662-3)

These are some of the same men who see great virtue in the collectivized, socialized society. They want vast powers concentrated in Washington. Samuel Adams of the founding fathers said this was the very thing Constitutional government was designed to prevent.

Arthur M. Schlesinger Jr., is another powerful influence in Washington and a former Presidential adviser. He not only advocates socialism for the United States but believes that we could eventually form a permanent alliance with Communism. He says this would be achieved by having America move to the left while the Communists move to the right. We would then meet at the vital center of the socialist-left. The American Constitution, of course, would automatically be discarded. Arthur Schlesinger and his associates are also opposed to the liberation of the captive nations, even if these nations do it by themselves. These men do not look upon Communism as an enemy. They consider Communist leaders to be over-zealous allies who will mellow. Therefore, they believe in containing Communism, but otherwise supporting it, not short of thwarting it. They further recommend that wherever Communists or Socialists regimes are collapsing, we should prop them up, feed them, trade with them, grant them loans on long term credits.

From reading the daily paper, you will know that the ideas of these men have, unfortunately, already been adopted by Washington as the official policy of the United States.

Now I would say in the great free country like ours, if these men advocate these suicidal and often treasonable doctrines shouldn't every patriotic American be free to speak out against them?

At this particular moment in history the United States Constitution is definitely threatened and every citizen should know about it. The warning of this hour should resound through the corridors of every American institution – schools, churches, the halls of Congress, press, radio and TV and so far as I am concerned and I am sure so far as you are concerned it will resound – with God's help.

Our Republic and Constitution are being destroyed while the enemies of freedom are being aided. How? In at least ten ways:

1. By diplomatic recognition and aid, trade and negotiations with the Communists.

2. By disarmament of our military defenses.

3. By destruction of our security laws and the promotion of atheism by decisions of the Supreme Court.

4. By loss of sovereignty and solvency to international commitments and membership in world organizations.

5. By undermining of local law enforcement agencies and Congressional investigation committees.

6. By usurpations by the Executive and the Judicial branches of our Federal Government.

7. By lawlessness in the name of civil rights.

8. By staggering national debt with inflation and the corruption of the currency.

9. By a multiplicity of executive orders and federal programs which greatly weaken local and state government.

10. By the sacrificing of American manhood by engaging in wars we apparently have no intention of winning.

Wherever possible, I have tried to speak out. It is for this very reason that certain people in Washington have bitterly criticized me. They don't want people to hear the message. It embarrasses them. The things which are destroying the Constitution are the things they have been voting for. They are afraid for their political careers if these facts are pointed out. They therefore try to silence any who carry the message – anyone who will stand up and be counted.

But these liberal politicians are not the only ones who are trying to silence the warning voice of American patriots. Moscow is equally alarmed.

It was in 1960 when the Communist leaders first decided to do something drastic about the rising tide of patriotism in the United States. The loss of Cuba to the Soviet Union had alerted many Americans. Citizens were holding study groups, seminars and freedom schools. The more they studied the more they realized how fast Communism was advancing on all fronts. They also learned to their amazement that most Washington politicians were doing practically nothing about it. In fact in many cases they were doing things to promote Communism. So the protests began to pour into the national capital from every state in the union. All over America there was an awakening.

The Soviet leaders knew this trend could create a crisis for Communism, not only in the United States, but elsewhere.

Therefore, they called together Communist delegates from eighty-one countries and held a meeting in Moscow.

In December, 1960, just five years ago – this Communist convention issued an edict that the rising tide of patriotism and anti-communism must be smashed. Especially in the United States. All the tricks of hate propaganda and smear tactics were to be unleashed on the heads of American patriots.

Now if the communists had been forced to do this job themselves, it would have been another failure. Americans would have simply closed ranks and united. But what mixes up so many people is the fact that the attack on patriotism and the smear of the anti–Communist movement did not come in the name of Moscow. It came in the name of influential Americans who espoused the Socialist-Communist line.

This was a minority block of liberals, American liberals, who formed a propaganda coalition with the Communists. Their strategy was ingenious. Almost over night they drew the fire away from the Communist Conspiracy and focused the heat of attack on the patriots.

How did they do it? They did it by saying that they were against the Communists but also against the anti-Communists. They said one was as bad as the other.

Now what kind of logic was this? What if we had taken this approach in the fight against Nazism? Informed patriots recognized it as confusion compounded by delusion. In any event, this deceptive line of propaganda had its impact. These liberal voices would denounce Communism and then turn right around and parrot the Communist line. They claimed they were anti-Communists, but spend most of their time fighting those who were really effective anti-Communists.

As I asked some of them at the time, "Are you fighting the communists or not? You claim to be fighting the fire, but you spend nearly all your time fighting the firemen!"

By 1962 these American liberals had almost completely neutralized the resurgence of American patriotism. They had frightened uninformed citizens away from study groups and patriotic rallies. They had made it popular to call patriotism a "controversial" subject which should not be discussed in school assemblies or churches.

From Washington, D.C., the FCC (Federal Communications Commission) issued an edict to radio and television stations that if they allowed the controversial subjects of "Americanism," "anti-Communism," or "States' Rights" to be discussed on their stations they would be required to give equal time, free of charge, to anyone wishing to present an opposite view.

Can you imagine this happening in a free country? I said to my family, "It is fantastic that anything like this could have happened in America."

Now we should all be opposed to Socialistic-Communism, for it is our mortal and spiritual enemy – the greatest evil in the world today. But the reason many liberals don't want the American people to form study groups to really understand and than fight Socialistic-Communism is that once the American people get the facts they will begin to realize that much of what these liberals advocate is actually helping the enemy.

The liberals hope you'll believe them when they tell you how anti-Communist they are. But they become alarmed if you really inform yourself on the subject of Socialistic-Communism. For after you inform yourself you might begin to study the liberal voting record. And this study would show you how much the liberals are giving aid and comfort to the enemy and how much the liberals are actually leading America towards Socialism itself.

For Communism is just another form of socialism, as is fascism. So now you can see the picture. These liberals want you to know how much they are doing for you – with your tax money of course. But they don't want you to realize that the path they are pursuing is socialistic, and that socialism is the same as communism in its ultimate effect on our liberties. When you point this out they want to shut you up – they accuse you of maligning them, of casting aspersions, of being political. No matter whether they label their bottle as liberalism, progressivism, or social reform – I know the contents of the bottle is poison to this Republic and I'm going to call it poison.

We do not need to question the motive of these liberals. They could be most sincere. But sincerity or supposed benevolence or even cleverness is not the question. The question is: "Are we going to save this country from the hands of the enemy and the deceived?"

As J. Edgar Hoover said, "A tragedy of the past generation in the United States is that so many persons, including high-ranking statesmen, public officials, educators, ministers of the Gospel, professional men have been duped into helping communism. Communist leaders have proclaimed that Communism must be partly built with non-Communist hands, and this, to a large extent, is true." (Masters of Deceit, p. 93)

"We cannot defeat Communism with socialism, nor with secularism, nor with pacifism, nor with appeasement or accommodation. We can only defeat Communism with true Americanism." (Address by J. Edgar Hoover, Oct. 9, 1962)

So from the very beginning of this Moscow campaign, to stop the anti-Communist movement in this country, it was an important part of the Communist strategy to get their liberal American friends to carry out an attack against patriotic organizations. Of course, the Communists have learned not to attack all patriotic groups at once. Their strategy is to focus on just one organization and make it so detestable and ugly in the public mind that they can hold it up as a sort of a tar baby and then use it to smear all other individuals or groups in the same category.

It was interesting to see just where the Communists would begin their dirty work; which organization would be singled out to get the tar brush treatment. It could have been the American Farm Bureau which the Communists have consistently denounced. It could have been the American Legion, Veterans of Foreign Wars, the DAR, the Sons of the American Revolution. These have been favorite Communist targets in the past as had J. Edgar Hoover and the FBI.

As it turned out, it was none of these. Instead, the Communists chose to focus their attack on a fairly new organization which very few people had heard about, including myself. They decided to level practically their entire arsenal on The John Birch society. For the non-political Birch Society had within it, both the policy, the program and the personnel to help defeat the Conspiracy in this country. And the communists knew it, for they had seen its results.

On February 25, 1961 the official Communist paper in California, *The People's World*, came out with the opening blast. It said there is a new secret, fascist society which is setting up "cells" all over the United States. They said it was the most serious threat to the American way of life.

That was the signal for the bloc of American liberals to pick up the torch, and they did. Overnight the patriotic campaign against Communism was almost completely forgotten as the liberal vigilantes heroically rode out in full force to save the country from the "terrible Birchers."

Not only the ultra-liberal forces rallied to the battle, but some of the most respected conservative press took up the hue and cry, and many prominent, highly respected Americans also fell for the deceptive line.

The Communists had intended to confuse the American people and they did. The tar brush tactic smeared the image of the new, small, but rapidly growing John Birch Society to the point where many people thought it must be a group of neo-Nazis or a revival of the Ku Klux Klan. Some prominent, highly respected men who were so deceived that they declared that the infiltration of The John Birch society was equally bad as the infiltration of the Godless Communist Conspiracy.

From the beginning of this attack The John Birch Society pleaded for some kind of official investigation so the truth about them could be given to the public. They believed this was the only way they could counteract the tidal wave of false propaganda which was being heaped upon them. But the investigation was so long in coming that the purposes of the Communist-liberal coalition were completely accomplished. It will probably be a long time before the official report on The John Birch Society gets an honest hearing. This investigation was conducted by trained investigators who were working for the California Senate Fact-Finding Subcommittee on Un-American Activities. The investigation took two years. Sworn affidavits were obtained from scores of people. The attacks on the Society were studied. Interviews were conducted with detractors and supporters of the society. Undetected investigators attended Birch meetings. The Senate Fact-Finding report was issued in June, 1963.

But even this report was recklessly distorted by some of the liberal press stories. I therefore obtained a copy of the report myself so I could see what was in it. The report is sixty-two pages long, was signed by all members of the Committee, and was issued by the President Pro Tem of the California Senate, Senator Hugh M. Burns, a Democrat.

Here are a few quotes from the report.

"The society had been publicly charged with being a secret, fascist, subversive, un-American, anti–Semitic organization. We have not found any of these accusations to be supported by the evidence."

And a further quote from the report.

"We believe that the reason the John Birch Society has attracted so many members is that it simply appeared to them to be the most effective, indeed the only organization through which they could join a national movement to learn the truth about the Communist menace and than take some positive, concerted action to prevent its spread."

This report also goes on to verify what I have already told you, namely, that the attack against The John Birch Society commenced with an article in the *People's World*, California Communist paper.

Now in the light of what I have just related, you will understand my feelings when people would ask how I felt about The John Birch Society because of the amazingly effective propaganda against them, it has been very unpopular to defend this group. I can remember when it was unpopular to defend my own Church. Nevertheless, as soon as I learned what the Communists and liberals were doing to The John Birch Society, I felt a deep indignation that this should happen to any non–political, patriotic group of American citizens. I felt it was dishonest, immoral and crass hypocrisy. I still feel that way.

One liberal Congressman attacked the Society claiming it was "rotten to the core." Other influential liberals said they objected to the Society's "methods." If it was rotten to the core the California Senate Fact–Finding investigators couldn't discover it.

Some of the finest and best informed Americans I know have endorsed the Society and its program including a number of former FBI agents and officials, counterspies, intelligence and security officers, and so on. Many nationally prominent patriotic Americans serve without pay on its Council. As to its "methods" the report described the Society as a study group organization designed to "first learn the facts about Communism and than implement that knowledge with effective and responsible action." (p. 37) Now what is wrong with such methods as these? It was Communists and American liberals who objected to these "methods" because they were effective. They turned out to be traditional American methods that I could find no fault with.

Even in my own church I found a certain amount of confusion. I heard people say that the LDS church was opposed to The John Birch Society. This may come, in part at least, as a result of a statement made by the First Presidency three years ago. However, when President McKay discovered that this statement was being misinterpreted and certain people were quoting it to try and prove the LDS Church was opposing The John Birch Society, he authorized a clarifying statement.

This statement appeared in the official Church newspaper for March 16, 1963, and says "The church is not opposing The John Birch Society or any organization of like nature." And "that members of the Church are free to join anti-Communist organizations". The statement also says that only one man, President David O. McKay, speaks for the Church of Jesus Christ of Latter-day Saints on matters of policy.

Just as a matter of interest you may like to know in a few words what The John Birch Society is and what it stands for so that you will have a little better idea why some of us have risen to its defense. Actually what would be better for you to do would be to read some of their literature for yourself. Everything the Birch Society publishes is available to member and non-member alike and their headquarters at Belmont Massachusetts 02178 will be happy to provide this literature including some other free introductory material.

The society takes its name from one of the greatest heroes of World War II, Captain John Birch, who was murdered by the Chinese Communists ten days after the war.

The society attempts through an educational and monthly action program to use every legal and moral means practicable to preserve our inspired Constitution. These programs have had a real impact against the Conspiracy. The various programs are purely suggestive and the members are cautioned never to do anything that goes contrary to their conscience and judgment.

The Society is not a political organization – It never endorses a candidate or contributes to candidates. It encourages its members, whether they be Democrats, Republicans or Independents to study the issues and candidates in the light of our Constitution, and the threats to it, and then govern themselves accordingly.

Among other things the Society is for a balanced budget, for the Monroe Doctrine and for letting the states solve their own problems.

It is against foreign aid to the Communists, against the Marxist graduated income tax and against the Federal Government competing with tax paying free enterprise. In a sentence, The John Birch Society believes in less centralized government, more personal responsibility and a better world.

I do not belong to The John Birch Society, but I have always defended this group, just as I do not belong to but have defended the American Farm Bureau, the DAR, the American Legion, the Veterans of Foreign Wars and any other patriotic group trying to alert Americans to the Socialist–Communist threat. I have also defended J. Edgar Hoover and the FBI.

When my son Reed was invited to be a state coordinator for The John Birch Society, he asked me if he should accept it. I had read the Blue Book and other basic materials of the Society. I had met Mr. Welch and other leaders and members. I had read Mr. Welch's famous letter which has since been published in book form entitled *The Politician*. I knew Reed would be enrolling in an unpopular cause. I also knew he would receive a certain amount of vilification if he took this job. Nevertheless, I told him to go ahead if he thought this was a most effective way to defend the Constitution and fight the Socialist-Communist menace. I would have given him equal encouragement if he had been considering the FBI or any of our national patriotic organizations dedicated to the fight against the Godless Conspiracy which threatens all we hold dear.

When he joined I expressed my opinion that I was convinced that The John Birch Society was the most effective non-Church organization in our fight against creeping socialism and Godless communism. I also stated that I admired Reed's courage and applauded his decision.

Some people, I'm sure well meaning, have told me this was not good strategy, but I disagree. I feel it is always good strategy to stand up for the right, even when it is unpopular. Perhaps I should say, especially when it is unpopular.

I had to make this same decision all over again when President David O. McKay received an invitation from former Congressman John Rousselot, asking that I be authorized to give a patriotic speech at a testimonial dinner for Robert Welch. President McKay after careful consideration, told me I should make the talk and that I had his permission and blessing. And so the invitation was accepted.

This talk was given at the Hollywood Palladium, September 23rd, 1963. Nearly 2,000 heard my talk that night and 4,000 Kiwanians heard a similar message the following day when I spoke at their annual convention.

Both talks dealt with the preservation of the Constitution and the need to resist the Communist threat. At the Welch Testimonial dinner I commended The John Birch Society and encouraged them to protect the principles of liberty throughout the land.

Of course, as all of you know, this talk brought an immediate outcry from some liberal elements in Washington. These voices said that I, as a Church official, had no business speaking at the Robert Welch dinner. They said it was making me "controversial." Patrick Henry and the Founding Fathers were also "controversial," as true patriots have ever been. Perhaps they did not realize that I had fulfilled this assignment with the full approval of President McKay. And perhaps they did not realize that President David O. McKay has not hesitated to speak out for freedom even if some people have considered such patriotism as "controversial." And neither will I hesitate. The fight to save the Constitution is not mere controversy, nor the fight against Communism. In fact, it is a war with the devil – Christ verses anti-Christ – and I am willing to fight it. It is a fight against the greatest evil in this world – a ruthless, powerful, godless conspiracy.

J Edgar Hoover has warned that the cold war is a real war and that the threat is increasing. I agree, and unfortunately we are losing the war.

I think it is time for every patriotic American to join with neighbors to study the Constitution and the Conspiracy. Subscribe to several good patriotic magazines such as *American Opinion*. Buy a few basic books, such as *Masters of Deceit* and *A Study of Communism* by J. Edgar Hoover; *The Naked Communist* by Cleon Skousen, recommended by President David O. McKay, in the General Conference of the Church, October 1959; *You Can Trust the Communists* by Dr. Fred Schwartz, and so on. And then prepare to do some independent thinking. And remember that the organized who have a plan and are dedicated though they be few, will always defeat the many who are not organized and who lack plans and dedication. The communists know this and have proven it. Isn't it about time that most Americans realize it too?

In conclusion may I say that one of our most serious problems is the inferiority complex which people feel when they are not informed and unorganized. They dare not make a decision on these vital issues. They let other people think for them. They stumble around in the middle of the road trying to avoid being "controversial" and get hit by traffic going both ways.

To the patriots I say this: Take that long eternal look. Stand up for freedom no matter what the cost.
It can help to save your soul – and maybe your country.
This is a choice land....choice above all others. Blessed by the Almighty, our forefathers have made and kept it so. It will continue to be a land of freedom and liberty as long as we are able to advance in the light of sound and enduring principles of right. To sacrifice such principles for momentary expediency – often selfishly motivated – is to endanger our noble heritage and is unworthy of this great American people.
With all my heart I love this great nation. I have lived and traveled abroad just enough to make me appreciate rather fully what we have here. To me this is not just another nation. It is not just one of a family of nations. This is a nation with a great mission to perform for the benefit and blessing of liberty–loving people everywhere. It is my firm conviction that The Constitution of this land was established by men whom the God of heaven raised up unto that very purpose. This is part of my religious faith.
The days ahead are sobering and challenging, and will demand the faith, prayers and loyalty of every American. As the ancient apostle declared:
"The night is far spent, the day is at hand; let us therefore cast off the works of darkness, and let us put on the armour of light." (Romans 13:12)

May God give us the wisdom to recognize the dangers of complacency, the threat to our freedom and the strength to meet this danger courageously.

Our challenge is to keep America strong and free – strong socially, strong economically, and, above all, strong spiritually, if our way of life is to endure. There is no other way. Only in this course is there safety for our nation.

In this mighty struggle each of you has a part. Every person on the earth today chose the right side during the war in heaven. Be on the right side now. Stand up and be counted. If you get discouraged remember the words of Edward Everett Hale when he said:

"I am only one, but I am one.
I can't do everything, but I can do something.
What I can do, that I ought to do,
And what I ought to do,
By the grace of God, I shall do!"

And this is my prayer for you this day. May God bless all of you, each and every one. Thank you very much.

THE PROPER ROLE OF GOVERNMENT

Men in the public spotlight constantly are asked to express an opinion on a myriad of government proposals and projects. "What do you think of TVA?" "What is your opinion of Medicare?" How do you feel about Urban Renewal?" The list is endless. All too often, answers to these questions seem to be based, not upon any solid principle, but upon the popularity of the specific government program in question. Seldom are men willing to oppose a popular program if they, themselves, wish to be popular – especially if they seek public office.

Government Should Be Based Upon Sound Principles
Such an approach to vital political questions of the day can only lead to public confusion and legislative chaos. Decisions of this nature should be based upon and measured against certain basic principles regarding the proper role of government. If principles are correct, then they can be applied to any specific proposal with confidence.

"Are there not, in reality, underlying, universal principles with reference to which all issues must be resolved whether the society be simple or complex in its mechanical organization? It seems to me we could relieve ourselves of most of the bewilderment which so unsettles and distracts us by subjecting each situation to the simple test of right and wrong. Right and wrong as moral principles do not change. They are applicable and reliable determinants whether the situations with which we deal are simple or complicated. There is always a right and wrong to every question which requires our solution." (Jerreld L. Newquist, Prophets, Principles and National Survival, p. 21–22)

Unlike the political opportunist, the true statesman values principle above popularity, and works to create popularity for those political principles which are wise and just.

The Correct Role Of Government

I should like to outline in clear, concise, and straight-forward terms the political principles to which I subscribe. These are the guidelines which determine, now and in the future, my attitudes and actions toward all domestic proposals and projects and projects of government. These are the principles which, in my opinion, proclaim the proper role of government in the domestic affairs of the nation.

"(I) believe that governments were instituted of God for the benefit of man; and that he holds men accountable for their acts in relation to them, both in making laws and administering them, for the good and safety of society."

"(I) believe that no government can exist in peace, except such laws are framed and held inviolate as will secure to each individual the free exercise of conscience, the right and control of property, and the protection of life…"

"(I) believe that all men are bound to sustain and uphold the respective governments in which they reside, while protected in their inherent and inalienable rights by the laws of such governments; and that sedition and rebellion are unbecoming every citizen thus protected, and should be punished accordingly; and that all governments have a right to enact such laws as in their own judgments are best calculated to secure the public interest; at the same time, however, holding sacred the freedom of conscience."

The Most Important Function Of Government

It is generally agreed that the most important single function of government is to secure the rights and freedoms of individual citizens. But, what are those right? And what is their source? Until these questions are answered there is little likelihood that we can correctly determine how government can best secure them. Thomas Paine, back in the days of the American Revolution, explained that:

"Rights are not gifts from one man to another, nor from one class of men to another... It is impossible to discover any origin of rights other than in the origin of man; it consequently follows that rights appertain to man in right of his existence, and must therefore be equal to every man." (P.P.N.S., p. 134)

The great Thomas Jefferson asked:

"Can the liberties of a nation be thought secure when we have removed their only firm basis, a conviction in the minds of the people that these liberties are of the gift of God? That they are not to be violated but with his wrath?" (Works 8:404; P.P.N.S., p.141)

Starting at the foundation of the pyramid, let us first consider the origin of those freedoms we have come to know are human rights. There are only two possible sources. Rights are either God-given as part of the Divine Plan, or they are granted by government as part of the political plan. Reason, necessity, tradition and religious convictions all lead me to accept the divine origin of these rights. If we accept the premise that human rights are granted by government, then we must be willing to accept the corollary that they can be denied by government. I, for one, shall never accept that premise. As the French political economist, Frederick Bastiat, phrased it so succinctly, "Life, liberty, and property do not exist because men have made laws. On the contrary, it was the fact that life, liberty, and property existed beforehand that caused men to make laws in the first place." (The Law, p.6)

The Real Meaning Of The Separation Of Church And State

I support the doctrine of separation of church and state as traditionally interpreted to prohibit the establishment of an official national religion. But I am opposed to the doctrine of separation of church and state as currently interpreted to divorce government from any formal recognition of God. The current trend strikes a potentially fatal blow at the concept of the divine origin of our rights, and unlocks the door for an easy entry of future tyranny. If Americans should ever come to believe that their rights and freedoms are instituted among men by politicians and bureaucrats, then they will no longer carry the proud inheritance of their forefathers, but will grovel before their masters seeking favors and dispensations – a throwback to the Feudal System of the Dark Ages. We must ever keep in mind the inspired words of Thomas Jefferson, as found in the Declaration of Independence:

"We hold these truths to be self-evident, that all men are created equal, that they are endowed by their Creator with certain unalienable Rights, that among these are Life, Liberty and the pursuit of Happiness. That to secure these rights, Governments are instituted among Men, deriving their just powers from the consent of the governed." (P.P.N. S., p.519)

Since God created man with certain unalienable rights, and man, in turn, created government to help secure and safeguard those rights, it follows that man is superior to the creature which he created. Man is superior to government and should remain master over it, not the other way around. Even the non-believer can appreciate the logic of this relationship.

The Source Of Governmental Power

Leaving aside, for a moment, the question of the divine origin of rights, it is obvious that a government is nothing more or less than a relatively small group of citizens who have been hired, in a sense, by the rest of us to perform certain functions and discharge certain responsibilities which have been authorized. It stands to reason that the government itself has no innate power or privilege to do anything. Its only source of authority and power is from the people who have created it. This is made clear in the Preamble to the Constitution of the United States, which reads: "We the people… do ordain and establish this Constitution for the United States of America."

The important thing to keep in mind is that the who have created their government can give to that government only such powers as they, themselves, have in the first place. Obviously, they cannot give that which they do not possess. So, the question boils down to this. What powers properly belong to each and every person in the absence of and prior to the establishment of any organized governmental form? A hypothetical question? Yes, indeed! But, it is a question which is vital to an understanding of the principles which underlie the proper function of government.

Of course, as James Madison, sometimes called the Father of the Constitution, said, "If men were angels, no government would be necessary. If angels were to govern men, neither external nor internal controls on government would be necessary." (The Federalist, No. 51)

Natural Rights

In a primitive state, there is no doubt that each man would be justified in using force, if necessary, to defend himself against physical harm, against theft of the fruits of his labor, and against enslavement by another. This principle was clearly explained by Bastiat:

"Each of us has a natural right – from God – to defend his person, his liberty, and his property. These are the three basic requirements of life, and the preservation of any one of them is completely dependent upon the preservation of the other two. For what are our faculties but the extension of our individuality? And what is property but an extension of our faculties?" (The Law, p.6)

Indeed, the early pioneers found that a great deal of their time and energy was being spent doing all three – defending themselves, their property and their liberty – in what properly was called the "Lawless West." In order for man to prosper, he cannot afford to spend his time constantly guarding his family, his fields, and his property against attack and theft, so he joins together with his neighbors and hires a sheriff. At this precise moment, government is born. The individual citizens delegate to the sheriff their unquestionable right to protect themselves. The sheriff now does for them only what they had a right to do for themselves–nothing more. Quoting again from Bastiat:

"If every person has the right to defend – even by force – his person, his liberty, and his property, then it follows that a group of men have the right to organize and support a common force to protect these rights constantly. Thus the principle of collective right – its reason for existing, its lawfulness – is based on individual right." (The Law, p. 6)

So far so good. But now we come to the moment of truth. Suppose pioneer "A" wants another horse for his wagon, He doesn't have the money to buy one, but since pioneer "B" has an extra horse, he decides that he is entitled to share in his neighbor's good fortune, Is he entitled to take his neighbor's horse? Obviously not! If his neighbor wishes to give it or lend it, that is another question. But so long as pioneer "B" wishes to keep his property, pioneer "A" has no just claim to it.

If "A" has no proper power to take "B's" property, can he delegate any such power to the sheriff? No. Even if everyone in the community desires that "B" give his extra horse to "A", they have no right individually or collectively to force him to do it. They cannot delegate a power they themselves do not have. This important principle was clearly understood and explained by John Locke nearly 300 years ago:

"For nobody can transfer to another more power than he has in himself, and nobody has an absolute arbitrary power over himself, or over any other, to destroy his own life, or take away the life of property of another." (Two Treatises of Civil Government, II, 135; P.P.N.S. p. 93)

The Proper Function Of Government

This means, then, that the proper function of government is limited only to those spheres of activity within which the individual citizen has the right to act. By deriving its just powers from the governed, government becomes primarily a mechanism for defense against bodily harm, theft and involuntary servitude. It cannot claim the power to redistribute the wealth or force reluctant citizens to perform acts of charity against their will. Government is created by man. No man possesses such power to delegate. The creature cannot exceed the creator.

In general terms, therefore, the proper role of government includes such defensive activities, as maintaining national military and local police forces for protection against loss of life, loss of property, and loss of liberty at the hands of either foreign despots or domestic criminals.

The Powers Of A Proper Government

It also includes those powers necessarily incidental to the protective functions such as:

(1) The maintenance of courts where those charged with crimes may be tried and where disputes between citizens may be impartially settled.

(2) The establishment of a monetary system and a standard of weights and measures so that courts may render money judgments, taxing authorities may levy taxes, and citizens may have a uniform standard to use in their business dealings.

My attitude toward government is succinctly expressed by the following provision taken from the Alabama Constitution:

"That the sole object and only legitimate end of government is to protect the citizen in the enjoyment of life, liberty, and property, and when the government assumes other functions it is usurpation and oppression." (Art. 1, Sec. 35)

An important test I use in passing judgment upon an act of government is this: If it were up to me as an individual to punish my neighbor for violating a given law, would it offend my conscience to do so? Since my conscience will never permit me to physically punish my fellow man unless he has done something evil, or unless he has failed to do something which I have a moral right to require of him to do, I will never knowingly authorize my agent, the government to do this on my behalf. I realize that when I give my consent to the adoption of a law, I specifically instruct the police – the government – to take either the life, liberty, or property of anyone who disobeys that law. Furthermore, I tell them that if anyone resists the enforcement of the law, they are to use any means necessary – yes, even putting the lawbreaker to death or putting him in jail – to overcome such resistance. These are extreme measures but unless laws are enforced, anarchy results. As John Locke explained many years ago:

"The end of law is not to abolish or restrain, but to preserve and enlarge freedom. For in all the states of created beings, capable of laws, where there is no law there is no freedom. For liberty is to be free from restraint and violence from others, which cannot be where there is no law; and is not, as we are told, 'a liberty for every man to do what he lists.' For who could be free, when every other man's humor might domineer over him? But a liberty to dispose and order freely as he lists his person, actions, possessions, and his whole property within the allowance of those laws under which he is, and therein not to be subject to the arbitrary will of another, but freely follow his own." (Two Treatises of Civil Government, II, 57: P.P.N.S., p.101)

I believe we Americans should use extreme care before lending our support to any proposed government program. We should fully recognize that government is no plaything. As George Washington warned, "Government is not reason, it is not eloquence – it is force! Like fire, it is a dangerous servant and a fearful master!" (The Red Carpet, p.142) It is an instrument of force and unless our conscience is clear that we would not hesitate to put a man to death, put him in jail or forcibly deprive him of his property for failing to obey a given law, we should oppose it.

The Constitution Of The United States

Another standard I use in deterring what law is good and what is bad is the Constitution of the United States. I regard this inspired document as a solemn agreement between the citizens of this nation which every officer of government is under a sacred duty to obey. As Washington stated so clearly in his immortal Farewell Address:

"The basis of our political systems is the right of the people to make and to alter their constitutions of government. But the constitution which at any time exists, until changed by an explicit and authentic act of the whole people, is sacredly obligatory upon all. The very idea of the power and the right of the people to establish government presupposes the duty of every individual to obey the established government." (P.P.N.S., p. 542)

I am especially mindful that the Constitution provides that the great bulk of the legitimate activities of government are to be carried out at the state or local level. This is the only way in which the principle of "self-government" can be made effective. As James Madison said before the adoption of the Constitution, " (We) rest all our political experiments on the capacity of mankind for self-government." (Federalist, No.39; P.P.N.S., p. 128) Thomas Jefferson made this interesting observation: "Sometimes it is said that man cannot be trusted with the government of himself. Can he, then, be trusted with the government of others? Or have we found angels in the forms of kings to govern him? Let history answer this question." (Works 8:3; P.P.N.S., p. 128)

The Value Of Local Government

It is a firm principle that the smallest or lowest level that can possibly undertake the task is the one that should do so. First, the community or city. If the city cannot handle it, then the county. Next, the state; and only if no smaller unit can possibly do the job should the federal government be considered. This is merely the application to the field of politics of that wise and time-tested principle of never asking a larger group to do that which can be done by a smaller group. And so far as government is concerned the smaller the unit and the closer it is to the people, the easier it is to guide it, to keep it solvent and to keep our freedom. Thomas Jefferson understood this principle very well and explained it this way:

"The way to have good and safe government, is not to trust it all to one, but to divide it among the many, distributing to every one exactly the functions he is competent to. Let the national government be entrusted with the defense of the nation, and its foreign and federal relations; the State governments with the civil rights, law, police, and administration of what concerns the State generally; the counties with the local concerns of the counties, and each ward direct the interests within itself. It is by dividing and subdividing these republics from the great national one down through all its subordinations, until it ends in the administration of every man's farm by himself; by placing under every one what his own eye may superintend, that all will be done for the best. What has destroyed liberty and the rights of man in every government which has ever existed under the sun? The generalizing and concentrating all cares and powers into one body." (Works 6:543; P.P.N.S., p. 125)

It is well to remember that the states of this republic created the Federal Government. The Federal Government did not create the states.

Things The Government Should Not Do

A category of government activity which, today, not only requires the closest scrutiny, but which also poses a grave danger to our continued freedom, is the activity not within the proper sphere of government. No one has the authority to grant such powers, as welfare programs, schemes for re-distributing the wealth, and activities which coerce people into acting in accordance with a prescribed code of social planning. There is one simple test. Do I as an individual have a right to use force upon my neighbor to accomplish this goal? If I do have such a right, then I may delegate that power to my government to exercise on my behalf. If I do not have that right as an individual, then I cannot delegate it to government, and I cannot ask my government to perform the act for me.

To be sure, there are times when this principle of the proper role of government is most annoying and inconvenient. If I could only force the ignorant to provided for themselves, or the selfish to be generous with their wealth! But if we permit government to manufacture its own authority out of thin air, and to create self-proclaimed powers not delegated to it by the people, then the creature exceeds the creator and becomes master. Beyond that point, where shall the line be drawn? Who is to say "this far, but no farther?" What clear principle will stay the hand of government from reaching farther and yet farther into our daily lives? We shouldn't forget the wise words of President Grover Cleveland that "... though the people support the Government the Government should not support the people." (P.P.N.S., p.345) We should also remember, as Frederic Bastiat reminded us, that "Nothing can enter the public treasury for the benefit of one citizen or one class unless other citizens and other classes have been forced to send it in." (The Law, p. 30; P.P.N.S., p. 350)

The Dividing Line Between Proper And Improper Government

As Bastiat pointed out over a hundred years ago, once government steps over this clear line between the protective or negative role into the aggressive role of redistributing the wealth and providing so-called "benefits" for some of its citizens, it then becomes a means for what he accurately described as legalized plunder. It becomes a lever of unlimited power which is the sought-after prize of unscrupulous individuals and pressure groups, each seeking to control the machine to fatten his own pockets or to benefit its favorite charities – all with the other fellow's money, of course. (The Law, 1850, reprinted by the Foundation for Economic Education, Irvington–On–Hudson, N.Y.)

The Nature Of Legal Plunder

Listen to Bastiat's explanation of this "legal plunder." "When a portion of wealth is transferred from the person who owns it – without his consent and without compensation, and whether by force or by fraud – to anyone who does not own it, then I say that property is violated; that an act of plunder is committed!

"How is the legal plunder to be identified? Quite simply. See if the law takes from some persons what belongs to them, and gives it to other persons to whom it does not belong. See if the law benefits one citizen at the expense of another by doing what the citizen himself cannot do without committing a crime..." (The Law, p. 21, 26; P.P.N.S., p. 377)

As Bastiat observed, and as history has proven, each class or special interest group competes with the others to throw the lever of governmental power in their favor, or at least to immunize itself against the effects of a previous thrust. Labor gets a minimum wage, so agriculture seeks a price support. Consumers demand price controls, and industry gets protective tariffs. In the end, no one is much further ahead, and everyone suffers the burdens of a gigantic bureaucracy and a loss of personal freedom. With each group out to get its share of the spoils, such governments historically have mushroomed into total welfare states. Once the process begins, once the principle of the protective function of government gives way to the aggressive or redistribute function, then forces are set in motion that drive the nation toward totalitarianism. "It is impossible," Bastiat correctly observed, "to introduce into society... a greater evil than this: the conversion of the law into an instrument of plunder." (The Law, p. 12)

Government Cannot Create Wealth

Students of history know that no government in the history of mankind has ever created any wealth. People who work create wealth.

James R. Evans, in his inspiring book, "The Glorious Quest" gives this simple illustration of legalized plunder:

"Assume, for example, that we were farmers, and that we received a letter from the government telling us that we were going to get a thousand dollars this year for plowed up acreage. But rather than the normal method of collection, we were to take this letter and collect $69.71 from Bill Brown, at such and such an address, and $82.47 from Henry Jones, $59.80 from a Bill Smith, and so on down the line; that these men would make up our farm subsidy. "Neither you nor I, nor would 99 percent of the farmers, walk up and ring a man's doorbell, hold out a hand and say, 'Give me what you've earned even though I have not.' We simply wouldn't do it because we would be facing directly the violation of a moral law, 'Thou shalt not steal.' In short, we would be held accountable for our actions."

The free creative energy of this choice nation "created more than 50% of all the world's products and possessions in the short span of 160 years. The only imperfection in the system is the imperfection in man himself." The last paragraph in this remarkable Evans book—which I commend to all—reads:

"No historian of the future will ever be able to prove that the ideas of individual liberty practiced in the United States of America were a failure. He may be able to prove that we were not yet worthy of them. The choice is ours." (Charles Hallberg and Co., 116 West Grand Avenue, Chicago, Illinois, 60610)

The Basic Error Of Marxism

According to Marxist doctrine, a human being is primarily an economic creature. In other words, his material well-being is all important; his privacy and his freedom are strictly secondary. The Soviet constitution reflects this philosophy in its emphasis on security: food, clothing, housing, medical care – the same things that might be considered in a jail. The basic concept is that the government has full responsibility for the welfare of the people and, in order to discharge that responsibility, must assume control of all their activities. It is significant that in actuality the Russian people have few of the rights supposedly "guaranteed" to them in their constitution, while the

American people have them in abundance even though they are not guaranteed. The reason, of course, is that material gain and economic security simply cannot be guaranteed by any government. They are the result and reward of hard work and industrious production. Unless the people bake one loaf of bread for each citizen, the government cannot guarantee that each will have one loaf to eat. Constitutions can be written, laws can be passed and imperial decrees can be issued, but unless the bread is produced, it can never be distributed.

The Real Cause Of American Prosperity

Why, then, do Americans bake more bread, manufacture more shoes and assemble more TV sets than Russians do? They do so precisely because our government does not guarantee these things. If it did, there would be so many accompanying taxes, controls, regulations and political manipulations that the productive genius that is America's would soon be reduced to the floundering level of waste and inefficiency now found behind the Iron Curtain. As Henry David Thoreau explained:

"This government never of itself furthered any enterprise, but by the alacrity with which it got out of its way. It does not educate. The character inherent in the American people has done all that has been accomplished; and it would have done somewhat more, if the government had not sometimes got in its way. For government is an expedient by which men would fain succeed in letting one another alone; and, as has been said, when it is most expedient, the governed are most let alone by it." (Quoted by Clarence B. Carson, The American Tradition, p. 100; P.P.N.S., p.171)

In 1801 Thomas Jefferson, in his First Inaugural Address, said:

"With all these blessings, what more is necessary to make us a happy and prosperous people? Still one thing more, fellow citizens – a wise and frugal government, which shall restrain men from injuring one another, which shall leave them otherwise free to regulate their own pursuits of industry and improvement, and shall not take from the mouth of labor the bread it had earned." (Works 8:3)

A Formula For Prosperity

The principle behind this American philosophy can be reduced to a rather simple formula:

Economic security for all is impossible without widespread abundance. Abundance is impossible without industrious and efficient production. Such production is impossible without energetic, willing and eager labor. This is not possible without incentive.

Of all forms of incentive – the freedom to attain a reward for one's labors is the most sustaining for most people. Sometimes called the profit motive, it is simply the right to plan and to earn and to enjoy the fruits of your labor.

This profit motive diminishes as government controls, regulations and taxes increase to deny the fruits of success to those who produce. Therefore, any attempt through governmental intervention to redistribute the material rewards of labor can only result in the eventual destruction of the productive base of society, without which real abundance and security for more than the ruling elite is quite impossible.

An Example Of The Consequences Of Disregarding These Principles

We have before us currently a sad example of what happens to a nation which ignores these principles. Former FBI agent, Dan Smoot, succinctly pointed this out on his broadcast number 649, dated January 29, 1968, as follows:

"England was killed by an idea: the idea that the weak, indolent and profligate must be supported by the strong, industrious, and frugal – to the degree that tax-consumers will have a living standard comparable to that of taxpayers; the idea that government exists for the purpose of plundering those who work to give the product of their labor to those who do not work. The economic and social cannibalism produced by this communist-socialist idea will destroy any society which adopts it and clings to it as a basic principle–any society."

The Power Of True Liberty From Improper Governmental Interference

Nearly two hundred years ago, Adam Smith, the Englishman, who understood these principles very well, published his great book, *The Wealth of Nations*, which contains this statement:

"The natural effort of every individual to better his own condition, when suffered to exert itself with freedom and security, is so powerful a principle, that it is alone, and without any assistance, not only capable of carrying on the society to wealth and prosperity, but of surmounting a hundred impertinent obstructions with which the folly of human laws too often encumbers its operations; though the effect of these obstructions is always more or less either to encroach upon its freedom, or to diminish its security." (Vol. 2, Book 4, Chapt. 5, p. 126)

But What About The Needy?

On the surface this may sound heartless and insensitive to the needs of those less fortunate individuals who are found in any society, no matter how affluent. "What about the lame, the sick and the destitute? Is an often-voiced question. Most other countries in the world have attempted to use the power of government to meet this need. Yet, in every case, the improvement has been marginal at best and has resulted in the long run creating more misery, more poverty, and certainly less freedom than when government first stepped in. As Henry Grady Weaver wrote, in his excellent book, *The Mainspring of Human Progress*:

"Most of the major ills of the world have been caused by well-meaning people who ignored the principle of individual freedom, except as applied to themselves, and who were obsessed with fanatical zeal to improve the lot of mankind-in-the-mass through some pet formula of their own... The hard done by ordinary criminals, murderers, gangsters, and thieves is negligible in comparison with the agony inflicted upon human beings by the professional 'do-gooders' who attempt to set themselves up as gods on earth and who would ruthlessly force their views on all others – with the abiding assurance that the end justifies the means." (p. 40–1; P.P.N.S., p. 313)

The Better Way

By comparison, America traditionally has followed Jefferson's advice of relying on individual action and charity. The result is that the

United States has fewer cases of genuine hardship per capita than any other country in the entire world or throughout all history. Even during the depression of the 1930's, Americans ate and lived better than most people in other countries do today.

What Is Wrong With A "Little" Socialism?

In reply to the argument that a little bit of socialism is good so long as it doesn't go too far, it is tempting to say that, in like fashion, just a little bit of theft or a little bit of cancer is all right, too! History proves that the growth of the welfare state is difficult to check before it comes to its full flower of dictatorship. But let us hope that this time around, the trend can be reversed. If not then we will see the inevitability of complete socialism, probably within our lifetime.

Three Reasons American Need Not Fall For Socialist Deceptions

Three factors may make a difference. First, there is sufficient historical knowledge of the failures of socialism and of the past mistakes of previous civilizations. Secondly, there are modern means of rapid communications to transmit these lessons of history to a large literate population. And thirdly, there is a growing number of dedicated men and women who, at great personal sacrifice, are actively working to promote a wider appreciation of these concepts. The timely joining together of these three factors may make it entirely possible for us to reverse the trend.

How Can Present Socialistic Trends Be Reversed?

This brings up the next question: How is it possible to cut out the various welfare-state features of our government which have already fastened themselves like cancer cells onto the body politic? Isn't drastic surgery already necessary, and can it be performed without endangering the patient? In answer, it is obvious that drastic measures are called for. No half–way or compromise actions will suffice. Like all surgery, it will not be without discomfort and perhaps even some scar tissue for a long time to come. But it must be done if the patient is to be saved, and it can be done without undue risk.

Obviously, not all welfare-state programs currently in force can be dropped simultaneously without causing tremendous economic and social upheaval. To try to do so would be like finding oneself at the controls of a hijacked airplane and attempting to return it by simply cutting off the engines in flight. It must be flown back, lowered in altitude, gradually reduced in speed and brought in for a smooth landing. Translated into practical terms, this means that the first step toward restoring the limited concept of government should be to freeze all welfare-state programs at their present level, making sure that no new ones are added. The next step would be to allow all present programs to run out their term with absolutely no renewal. The third step would involve the gradual phasing-out of those programs which are indefinite in their term. In my opinion, the bulk of the transition could be accomplished within a ten-year period and virtually completed within twenty years. Congress would serve as the initiator of this phase-out program, and the President would act as the executive in accordance with traditional constitutional procedures.

Summary Thus Far

As I summarize what I have attempted to cover, try to visualize the structural relationship between the six vital concepts that have made America the envy of the world. I have reference to the foundation of the divine origin of rights; limited government; the pillars of economic freedom and personal freedom, which result in abundance; followed by security and the pursuit of happiness.

America was built upon a firm foundation and created over many years from the bottom up. Other nations, impatient to acquire equal abundance, security and pursuit of happiness, rush headlong into that final phase of construction without building adequate foundations or supporting pillars. Their efforts are futile. And, even in our country, there are those who think that, because we now have the good things in life, we can afford to dispense with the foundations which have made them possible. They want to remove any recognition of God from governmental institutions. They want to expand the scope and reach of government which will undermine and erode our economic and personal freedoms. The abundance which is ours, the carefree existence which we have come to accept as a matter of course, can be toppled by these foolish experimenters and power seekers. By the grace of God, and with His help, we shall fence them off from the foundations of our liberty, and then begin our task of repair and construction.

As a conclusion to this discussion, I present a declaration of principles which have recently been prepared by a few American patriots, and to which I wholeheartedly subscribe.

Fifteen Principles Which Make For Good And Proper Government

As an Independent American for constitutional government I declare that:

(1) I believe that no people can maintain freedom unless their political institutions are founded upon faith in God and belief in the existence of moral law.

(2) I believe that God has endowed men with certain unalienable rights as set forth in the Declaration of Independence and that no legislature and no majority, however great, may morally limit or destroy these; that the sole function of government is to protect life, liberty, and property and anything more than this is usurpation and oppression.

(3) I believe that the Constitution of the United States was prepared and adopted by men acting under inspiration from Almighty God; that it is a solemn compact between the peoples of the States of this nation which all officers of government are under duty to obey; that the eternal moral laws expressed therein must be adhered to or individual liberty will perish.

(4) I believe it a violation of the Constitution for government to deprive the individual of either life, liberty, or property except for these purposes:

(a) Punish crime and provide for the administration of justice;

(b) Protect the right and control of private property;

(c) Wage defensive war and provide for the nation's defense;

(d) Compel each one who enjoys the protection of government to bear his fair share of the burden of performing the above functions.

(5) I hold that the Constitution denies government the power to take from the individual either his life, liberty, or property except in accordance with moral law; that the same moral law which governs the actions of men when acting alone is also applicable when they act in concert with others; that no citizen or group of citizens has any right to direct their agent, the government to perform any act which would be evil or offensive to the conscience if that citizen were performing the act himself outside the framework of government.

(6) I am hereby resolved that under no circumstances shall the freedoms guaranteed by the Bill of Rights be infringed. In particular I am opposed to any attempt on the part of the Federal Government to deny the people their right to bear arms, to worship and pray when and where they choose, or to own and control private property.

(7) I consider ourselves at war with international Communism which is committed to the destruction of our government, our right of property, and our freedom; that it is treason as defined by the Constitution to give aid and comfort to this implacable enemy.

(8) I am unalterably opposed to socialism, either in whole or in part, and regard it as an unconstitutional usurpation of power and a denial of the right of private property for government to own or operate the means of producing and distributing goods and services in competition with private enterprise, or to regiment owners in the legitimate use of private property.

(9) I maintain that every person who enjoys the protection of his life, liberty, and property should bear his fair share of the cost of government in providing that protection; that the elementary principles of justice set forth in the Constitution demand that all taxes imposed be uniform and that each person's property or income be taxed at the same rate.

(10) I believe in honest money, the gold and silver coinage of the Constitution, and a circulation medium convertible into such money without loss. I regard it as a flagrant violation of the explicit provisions of the Constitution for the Federal Government to make it a criminal offense to use gold or silver coin as legal tender or to use irredeemable paper money.

(11) I believe that each State is sovereign in performing those functions reserved to it by the Constitution and it is destructive of our federal system and the right of self-government guaranteed under the Constitution for the Federal Government to regulate or control the States in performing their functions or to engage in performing such functions itself.

(12) I consider it a violation of the Constitution for the Federal Government to levy taxes for the support of state or local government; that no State or local government can accept funds from the Federal Government and remain independent in performing its functions, nor can the citizens exercise their rights of self-government under such conditions.

(13) I deem it a violation of the right of private property guaranteed under the Constitution for the Federal Government to forcibly deprive the citizens of this nation of their nation of their property through taxation or otherwise, and make a gift thereof to foreign governments or their citizens.

(14) I believe that no treaty or agreement with other countries should deprive our citizens of rights guaranteed them by the Constitution.

(15) I consider it a direct violation of the obligation imposed upon it by the Constitution for the Federal Government to dismantle or weaken our military establishment below that point required for the protection of the States against invasion, or to surrender or commit our men, arms, or money to the control of foreign ore world organizations of governments. These things I believe to be the proper role of government.

We have strayed far afield. We must return to basic concepts and principles – to eternal verities. There is no other way. The storm signals are up. They are clear and ominous.

As Americans – citizens of the greatest nation under Heaven – we face difficult days. Never since the days of the Civil War – 100 years ago – has this choice nation faced such a crisis.

In closing I wish to refer you to the words of the patriot Thomas Paine, whose writings helped so much to stir into a flaming spirit the smoldering embers of patriotism during the days of the American Revolution:

"These are the times that try men's souls. The summer soldier and the sunshine patriot will in this crisis, shrink from the service of his country; but he that stands it now, deserves the love and thanks of man and woman. Tyranny, like hell, is not easily conquered; yet we have this consolation with us, that the harder the conflict, the more glorious the triumph. What we obtain too cheaply, we esteem too lightly; 'tis dearness only that gives everything its value. Heaven knows how to put a proper price upon its goods; and it would be strange indeed, if so celestial an article as freedom should not be highly rated." (The Political Works of Thomas Paine, p.55.)

I intend to keep fighting. My personal attitude is one of resolution–not resignation.

I have faith in the American people. I pray that we will never do anything that will jeopardize in any manner our priceless heritage. If we live and work so as to enjoy the approbation of a Divine Providence, we cannot fail. Without that help we cannot long endure.

All Right-Thinking Americans Should Now Take Their Stand

So I urge all Americans to put their courage to the test. Be firm in our conviction that our cause is just. Reaffirm our faith in all things for which true Americans have always stood.

I urge all Americans to arouse themselves and stay aroused. We must not make any further concessions to communism at home or abroad. We do not need to. We should oppose communism from our position of strength for we are not weak.

There is much work to be done. The time is short. Let us begin – in earnest – now and may God bless our efforts, I humbly pray.

CIVIC STANDARDS FOR THE FAITHFUL SAINTS

My beloved brothers and sisters, seen and unseen – and we are all brothers and sisters, children of the same Father in the spirit – humbly and gratefully I stand before you on this anniversary date of the organization of the restored church of Jesus Christ, 142 years ago. I love a general conference of the Church, except this particular part, and yet I rejoice in the opportunity to bear testimony to this, the greatest work in all the world.

Last fall I was invited by Baron von Blomberg, president of the United Religions Organization, to represent the Church as a guest of the king of Persia at the twenty-five hundredth anniversary of the founding of the Persian Empire by Cyrus the Great. Advised by the First Presidency to accept the invitation, I left immediately following the October conference to join with representatives of twenty-seven world religions, some fifty monarchs, and other notables at this historic celebration in Iran.

King Cyrus lived more than five hundred years before Christ and figured in prophecies of the Old Testament mentioned in 2 Chronicles and the book of Ezra, and by the prophets Ezekiel, Isaiah, and Daniel. The Bible states how "the Lord stirred up the spirit of Cyrus, King of Persia." (2 Chr. 36:22.) Cyrus restored certain political and social rights to the captive Hebrews, gave them permission to return to Jerusalem, and directed that Jehovah's temple should be rebuilt.

Parley P. Pratt, in describing the Prophet Joseph Smith, said that he had "the boldness, courage, temperance, perseverance and generosity of a Cyrus." (Autobiography of Parley Parker Pratt [Deseret Book Company, 1938], p. 46.)

President Wilford Woodruff said:

"Now I have thought many times that some of those ancient kings that were raised up, had in some respects more regard for the carrying out of some of these principles and laws, than even the Latter-day Saints have in our day. I will take as an ensample Cyrus. ... To trace the life of Cyrus from his birth to his death, whether he knew it or not, it looked as though he lived by inspiration in all his movements. He began with that temperance and virtue which would sustain any Christian country or any Christian king. ... Many of these principles followed him, and I have thought many of them were worthy, in many respects, the attention of men who have the Gospel of Jesus Christ." (Journal of Discourses, vol. 22, p. 207.)

God, the Father of us all, uses the men of the earth, especially good men, to accomplish his purposes. It has been true in the past, it is true today, it will be true in the future.

"Perhaps the Lord needs such men on the outside of His Church to help it along," said the late Elder Orson F. Whitney of the Quorum of the Twelve. "They are among its auxiliaries, and can do more good for the cause where the Lord has placed them, than anywhere else. ... Hence, some are drawn into the fold and receive a testimony of the truth; while others remain unconverted ... the beauties and glories of the gospel being veiled temporarily from their view, for a wise purpose. The Lord will open their eyes in His own due time. God is using more than one people for the accomplishment of His great and marvelous work. The Latter-day Saints cannot do it all. It is too vast, too arduous for any one people. ... We have no quarrel with the Gentiles. They are our partners in a certain sense." (Conference Report, April 1928, p. 59.)

This would certainly have been true of Colonel Thomas L. Kane, a true friend of the Saints in their dire need. It was true of General Doniphan, who, when ordered by his superior to shoot Joseph Smith, said: "It is cold blooded murder. I will not obey your order. ... and if you execute these men, I will hold you responsible before an earthly tribunal, so help me God." (Joseph Fielding Smith, Essentials in Church History, p. 241.)

We honor these partners because their devotion to correct principles overshadowed their devotion to popularity, party, or personalities.

We honor our founding fathers of this republic for the same reason. God raised up these patriotic partners to perform their mission, and he called them "wise men." (See D&C 101:80.) The First Presidency acknowledged that wisdom when they gave us the guideline a few years ago of supporting political candidates "who are truly dedicated to the Constitution in the tradition of our Founding Fathers." (Deseret News, November 2, 1964.) That tradition has been summarized in the book The American Tradition by Clarence Carson.

The Lord said that "the children of this world are in their generation wiser than the children of light." (Luke 16:8.) Our wise founders seemed to understand, better than most of us, our own scripture, which states that "it is the nature and disposition of almost all men, as soon as they get a little authority ... they will immediately begin to exercise unrighteous dominion." (D&C 121:39.)

To help prevent this, the founders knew that our elected leaders should be bound by certain fixed principles. Said Thomas Jefferson: "In questions of power then, let no more be heard of confidence in man but bind him down from mischief by the chains of the Constitution."

These wise founders, our patriotic partners, seemed to appreciate more than most of us the blessings of the boundaries that the Lord set within the Constitution, for he said, "And as pertaining to law of man, whatsoever is more or less than this, cometh of evil." (D&C 98:7.)

In God the founders trusted, and in his Constitution–not in the arm of flesh. "O Lord," said Nephi, "I have trusted in thee, and I will trust in thee forever. I will not put my trust in the arm of flesh; ... cursed is he that putteth his trust in man or maketh flesh his arm." (2 Ne. 4:34.)

President J. Reuben Clark, Jr., put it well when he said:

"God provided that in this land of liberty, our political allegiance shall run not to individuals, that is, to government officials, no matter how great or how small they may be. Under His plan our allegiance and the only allegiance we owe as citizens or denizens of the United States, runs to our inspired Constitution which God himself set up. So runs the oath of office of those who participate in government. A certain loyalty we do owe to the office which a man holds, but even here we owe just by reason of our citizenship, no loyalty to the man himself. In other countries it is to the individual that allegiance runs. This principle of allegiance to the Constitution is basic to our freedom. It is one of the great principles that distinguishes this 'land of liberty' from other countries." (Improvement Era, July 1940, p. 444.)

"Patriotism," said Theodore Roosevelt, "means to stand by the country. It does not mean to stand by the President or any other public official save exactly to the degree in which he himself stands by the country. ...

"Every man," said President Roosevelt, "who parrots the cry of 'stand by the President' without adding the proviso 'so far as he serves the Republic' takes an attitude as essentially unmanly as that of any Stuart royalist who championed the doctrine that the King could do no wrong. No self–respecting and intelligent free man could take such an attitude." (Theodore Roosevelt, Works, vol. 21, pp. 316, 321.) And yet as Latter-day Saints we should pray for our civic leaders and encourage them in righteousness.

"... to vote for wicked men, it would be sin," said Hyrum Smith. (Documentary History of the Church, vol. 6, p. 323.)

And the Prophet Joseph Smith said, "... let the people of the whole Union, like the inflexible Romans, whenever they find a promise made by a candidate that is not practiced as an officer, hurl the miserable sycophant from his exaltation. ..." (DHC, vol. 6, p. 207.)

Joseph and Hyrum's trust did not run to the arm of flesh, but to God and correct eternal principles. "I am the greatest advocate of the Constitution of the United States there is on the earth," said the Prophet Joseph Smith. (DHC, vol. 6, p. 56.)

The warning of President Joseph Fielding Smith is most timely: "Now I tell you it is time the people of the United States were waking up with the understanding that if they don't save the Constitution from the dangers that threaten it, we will have a change of government." (Conference Report, April 1950, p. 159.)

Another guideline given by the First Presidency was "to support good and conscientious candidates, of either party, who are aware of the great dangers" facing the free world. (Deseret News, November 2, 1964.)

Fortunately we have materials to help us face these threatening dangers in the writings of President David O. McKay and other church leaders. Some other fine sources by LDS authors attempting to awaken and inform us of our duty are: *Prophets, Principles, and National Survival* (Jerreld L. Newquist), *Many Are Called But Few Are Chosen* (H. Verlan Andersen), and *The Elders of Israel and the Constitution* (Jerome Horowitz).

But the greatest handbook for freedom in this fight against evil is the Book of Mormon.

This leads me to the second great civic standard for the Saints. For in addition to our inspired Constitution, we have the scriptures.

Joseph Smith said that the Book of Mormon was the "keystone of our religion" and the "most correct" book on earth. (DHC, vol. 6, p. 56.) This most correct book on earth states that the downfall of two great American civilizations came as a result of secret conspiracies whose desire was to overthrow the freedom of the people. "And they have caused the destruction of this people of whom I am now speaking," says Moroni, "and also the destruction of the people of Nephi." (Ether 8:21.)

Now undoubtedly Moroni could have pointed out many factors that led to the destruction of the people, but notice how he singled out the secret combinations, just as the Church today could point out many threats to peace, prosperity, and the spread of God's work, but it has singled out the greatest threat as the godless conspiracy. There is no conspiracy theory in the Book of Mormon – it is a conspiracy fact.

And along this line, I would highly recommend to you a new book entitled *None Dare Call it Conspiracy*, by Gary Allen.

Then Moroni speaks to us in this day and says, "Wherefore, the Lord commandeth you, when ye shall see these things come among you that ye shall awake to a sense of your awful situation, because of this secret combination which shall be among you" (Ether 8:14.)

The Book of Mormon further warns that "whatsoever nation shall uphold such secret combinations, to get power and gain, until they shall spread over the nation, behold they shall be destroyed. ..." (Ether 8:22.)

This scripture should alert us to what is ahead unless we repent, because there is no question but that as people of the free world, we are increasingly upholding many of the evils of the adversary today. By court edict godless conspirators can run for government office, teach in our schools, hold office in labor unions, work in our defense plants, serve in our merchant marines, etc. As a nation, we are helping to underwrite many evil revolutionaries in our country.

Now we are assured that the Church will remain on the earth until the Lord comes again – but at what price? The Saints in the early days were assured that Zion would be established in Jackson County, but look at what their unfaithfulness cost them in bloodshed and delay.

President Clark warned us that "we stand in danger of losing our liberties, and that once lost, only blood will bring them back; and once lost, we of this church will, in order to keep the Church going forward, have more sacrifices to make and more persecutions to endure than we have yet known. ..." (CR, April 1944, p. 116.) And he stated that if the conspiracy "comes here it will probably come in its full vigor and there will be a lot of vacant places among those who guide and direct, not only this government, but also this Church of ours." (CR, April 1952.)

Now the third great civic standard for the Saints is the inspired word of the prophets – particularly the living president, God's mouthpiece on the earth today. Keep your eye on the captain and judge the words of all lesser authority by his inspired counsel.

The story is told how Brigham Young, driving through a community, saw a man building a house and simply told him to double the thickness of his walls. Accepting President Young as a prophet, the man changed his plans and doubled the walls. Shortly afterward a flood came through that town, resulting in much destruction, but this man's walls stood. While putting the roof on his house, he was heard singing, "We thank thee, O God, for a prophet!"

Joseph Smith taught "that a prophet was a prophet only when he was acting as such." (DHC, vol. 5, p. 265.)

Suppose a leader of the Church were to tell you that you were supporting the wrong side of a particular issue. Some might immediately resist this leader and his counsel or ignore it, but I would suggest that you first apply the fourth great civic standard for the faithful Saints. That standard is to live for, to get, and then to follow the promptings of the Holy Spirit.

Said Brigham Young: "I am more afraid that this people have so much confidence in their leaders that they will not inquire for themselves of God whether they are led by Him. ... Let every man and woman know, by the whisperings of the Spirit of God to themselves, whether their leaders are walking in the path the Lord dictates, or not." (JD, vol. 9, p. 150.)

A number of years ago, because of a statement that appeared to represent the policy of the Church, a faithful member feared he was supporting the wrong candidate for public office. Humbly he took the matter up with the Lord. Through the Spirit of the Lord he gained the conviction of the course he should follow, and he dropped his support of this particular candidate.

This good brother, by fervent prayer, got the answer that in time proved to be the right course.

We urge all men to read the Book of Mormon and then ask God if it is true. And the promise is sure that they may know of its truthfulness through the Holy Ghost, "and by the power of the Holy Ghost [men] may know the truth of all things." (Moro. 10:5.)

We need the constant guidance of that Spirit. We live in an age of deceit. "O my people," said Isaiah in the Book of Mormon, "they who lead thee cause thee to err and destroy the way of thy paths." (2 Ne. 13:12.) Even within the Church we have been warned that "the ravening wolves are amongst us, from our own membership, and they, more than any others, are clothed in sheep's clothing, because they wear the habiliments of the priesthood." (J. Reuben Clark, Jr., CR, April 1949, p. 163.)

The Lord holds us accountable if we are not wise and are deceived. "For they that are wise," he said, "and have received the truth, and have taken the Holy Spirit for their guide, and have not been deceived–verily I say unto you, they shall not be hewn down and cast into the fire, but shall abide the day." (D&C 45:57.)

And so four great civic standards for the faithful Saints are, first, the Constitution ordained by God through wise men; second, the scriptures, particularly the Book of Mormon; third, the inspired counsel of the prophets, especially the living president, and fourth, the guidance of the Holy Spirit.

God bless us all that we may use these standards and by so doing bless ourselves, our families, our community, our nation, and the world, I humbly pray, as I bear my witness to the truth of this great Latter-day work, in the name of Jesus Christ. Amen.

UNITED STATES FOREIGN POLICY

"Observe good faith and justice towards all Nations; cultivate peace and harmony with all. Religion and Morality enjoin this conduct; and can it be, that good policy does not equally enjoin it? It will be worthy of a free, enlightened, and, at no distant period, a great Nation, to give to mankind the magnanimous and too novel example of a people always guided by an exalted justice and benevolence.

"... Can it be that Providence has not connected the permanent felicity of a Nation with its Virtue?"

President George Washington,
Farewell Address, September 17, 1796

In the "Virginia Bill of Rights," drafted by George Mason and adopted by the Virginia Convention on June 12, 1776, there appears this statement in Article 15:

"No free government, or the blessings of liberty, can be preserved to any people, but by a firm adherence to justice, moderation, temperance, frugality and virtue, and by frequent recurrence to fundamental principles." (Documents of American History, [Henry S. Commager, Editor], 1: 104)

"The paramount need today," recently wrote David Lawrence, "is for the United States to clear the air by emphasizing fundamental principles. Until there are acts that implement those principles—not just words—diplomacy will accomplish nothing and the world will remain continually on the brink of war." (U.S. News and World Report, January 27, 1964)

It has been truly said that:
"We cannot clean up the mess in Washington, balance the budget, reduce taxes, check creeping Socialism, tell what is muscle or fat in our sprawling rearmament programs, purge subversives from our State Department, unless we come to grips with our foreign policy, upon which all other policies depend." (Senator Robert A. Taft, quoted by Phyllis Schlafly, A Choice Not An Echo, p. 26)

Ever since World War I, when we sent American boys to Europe supposedly to "make the world safe for democracy," our leaders in Washington have been acting as though the American people elected them to office for the primary purpose of leading the entire planet toward international peace, prosperity and one–world government. At times, these men appear to be more concerned with something called world opinion or with their image as world leaders than they are with securing the best possible advantage for us, that they are not "nationalistic" in their views, that they are willing to sacrifice narrow American interests for the greater good of the world community. Patriotism and America-first have become vulgar concepts within the chambers of our State Department. It is no wonder that the strength and prestige of the United States has slipped so low everywhere in the world.

In this connection, it is well to remember that on June 25, 1787, during the formulation of the Constitution at the Philadelphia Convention, Charles Pinckney, of South Carolina, made the famous speech in which he asserted:
"We mistake the object of our Government, if we hope or wish that it is to make us respectable abroad. Conquest or superiority among other powers is not or ought not ever to be the object of republican systems. If they are sufficiently active & energetic to rescue us from

contempt & preserve our domestic happiness & security, it is all we can expect from them – it is more than almost any other Government ensures to its citizens." (The Records of the Federal Convention [Max Farrand, Editor], 1: 402)

In his book, A Foreign Policy for Americans, the late Senator Robert A. Taft correctly reasoned that:
"No one can think intelligently on the many complicated problems of American foreign policy unless he decides first what he considers the real purpose and object of that policy... There has been no consistent purpose in our foreign policy for a good many years past... Fundamentally, I believe the ultimate purpose of our foreign policy must be to protect the liberty of the people of the United States." (p. 11)

There is one and only one legitimate goal of United States foreign policy. It is a narrow goal, a nationalistic goal: the preservation of our national independence. Nothing in the Constitution grants that the President shall have the privilege of offering himself as a world leader. He's our executive; he's on our payroll, in necessary; he's supposed to put our best interests in front of those of other nations. Nothing in the Constitution nor in logic grants to the President of the United States or to Congress the power to influence the political life of other countries, to "uplift" their cultures, to bolster their economies, to feed their peoples or even to defend them against their enemies. This point was made clear by the wise father of our country, George Washington:
"I have always given it as my decided opinion that no nation has a right to intermeddle in the internal concerns of another; that every one had a right to form and adopt whatever government they liked best to live under them selves; and that if this country could, consistent with its engagements, maintain a strict neutrality and thereby preserve peace, it was bound to do so by motives of policy, interest, and every other consideration." (George Washington (1732–1799) Letter to James Monroe, 25 Aug. 1796)

The preservation of America's political, economic and military independence — the three cornerstones of sovereignty — is the sum and total prerogative of our government in dealing with the affairs of the world. Beyond that point, any humanitarian or charitable activities are the responsibility of individual citizens voluntarily without coercion of others to participate.

The proper function of government must be limited to a defensive role — the defense of individual citizens against bodily harm, theft and involuntary servitude at the hands of either domestic or foreign criminals. But to protect our people from bodily harm at the hands of foreign aggressors, we must maintain a military force which is not only capable of crushing an invasion, but of striking a sufficiently powerful counterblow as to make in unattractive for would-be conquerors to try their luck with us.

As President Washington explained in his Fifth Annual Address to both Houses of Congress:
"There is a rank due to the United States among nations, which will be withheld, if not absolutely lost, by the reputation of weakness. If we desire to avoid insult, we must be able to repel it; if we desire to secure the peace, one of the most powerful instruments of our rising prosperity, it must be known that we are at all times ready for war." (December 3, 1793; Writings 12:352)

He had earlier, in his First Annual Address, strongly warned that:
"To be prepared for war is one of the most effectual means of preserving peace. A free people ought not only to be armed, but disciplined." (January 8, 1790; Writings 11:456)

To protect our people from international theft, we must enter into agreements with other nations to abide by certain rules regarding trade, exchange of currency, enforcement of contracts, patent rights, etc. To protect our people against involuntary servitude or the loss of personal freedom on the international level, we must be willing to use our military might to help even one of our citizens no matter where he might be kidnapped or enslaved.

For those of you who have never heard or do not remember it, the story of Ion Perdicaris instructs us what an American President can and should do to protect the lives of its citizens. It seems that in the early years of the century, a North African bandit named Raisuli kidnapped Perdicaris, a naturalized American of Greek extraction.

Teddy Roosevelt was our President at that time, and he knew just what to do. He did not "negotiate." And he did not send any "urgent requests." He simply ordered one of our gunboats to stand offshore, and sent the local sultan the following telegram: "Perdicaris alive, or Raisuli dead." They say Raisuli didn't waste any time getting a healthy Perdicaris down to the dock. (Review of the News, February 7, 1968, pp. 20–21)

Certainly we must avoid becoming entangled in a web of international treaties whose terms and clauses might reach inside our own borders and restrict our freedoms here at home.[2]

This is the defensive role of government expressed in international terms. Interestingly enough, these three aspects of national defense also translate directly into the three aspects of national sovereignty: military, economic and political.

Applying this philosophy to the sphere of foreign policy, one is able almost instantly to determine the correct answer to so many international questions that, otherwise, seem hopelessly complex. If the preservation and strengthening of our military, economic and political independence is the only legitimate objective of foreign policy decisions, then, at last, those decisions can be directed by a brilliant beacon of light that unerringly guides our ship of state past the treacherous reefs of international intrigue and into a calm open sea.

Should we disarm? And does it really make any difference whether we disarm unilaterally or collaterally? Either course of action would surrender our military independence. Should we pool our economic resources or our monetary system with those of other nations to create some kind of regional common market? It would constitute the surrender of our economic independence. Should we enter into treaties such as the U.N. Covenants which would obligate our citizens to conform their social behavior, their educational practices to rules and regulations set down by international agencies? Such treaty obligations amount to the voluntary and piece-meal surrender of our political independence. The answer to all such questions is a resounding "no," for the simple reason that the only way America can survive in this basically hostile and topsy-turvy world is to remain militarily, economically and politically strong and independent.

We must put off our rose-colored glasses, quit repeating those soothing but entirely false statements about world unity and brotherhood, and look to the world as it is, not as we would like it to become. Such an objective, and perhaps painful, survey leads to but one conclusion. We would be committing national suicide to surrender any of our independence, and chain ourselves to other nations in such a sick and turbulent world. President George Washington, in his immortal Farewell Address, explained our true policy in this regard:

"The great rule of conduct for us, in regard to foreign nations, is in extending our commercial relations to have with them as little political connection as possible...'Tis our true policy to steer clear of permanent alliances, with any portion of the foreign world...Taking care always to keep ourselves, by suitable establishments on a respectably defensive posture, we may safely trust to temporary alliances for extraordinary emergencies." (September 17, 1796; Writings 13: 316–318; P.P.N.S., p. 547)

President Thomas Jefferson, in his First Inaugural Address, while discussing what he deemed to be "the essential principles of our government,"[3] explained that as far as our relations with foreign nations are concerned this means:

Equal and exact justice to all men, of whatever state or persuasion, religious or political; peace, commerce, and honest friendship with all nations – entangling alliances with none. . . (March 4, 1801; Works 8:4)

The world is smaller, you say? True, it is, but if one finds himself locked in a house with maniacs, thieves and murderers – even a small house – he does not increase his chances of survival by entering into alliances with his potential attackers and becoming dependent upon them for protection to the point where he is unable to defend himself. Perhaps the analogy between nations and maniacs is a little strong for some to accept. But if we put aside our squeamishness over strong language, and look hard at the real world in which we live, the analogy is quite sound in all but the rarest exceptions.

Already, I can hear the chorus chanting "Isolationism, isolationism, he's turning back the clock to isolationism." How many use that word without having the slightest idea of what it really means! The so-called isolationism of the United States in past decades is a pure myth. What isolationism? Long before the current trend of revoking our Declaration of Independence under the guise of international cooperation, American influence and trade was felt in every region of the globe. Individuals and private groups spread knowledge, business, prosperity, religion, good will and, above all, respect throughout every foreign continent. It was not necessary then for America to give up her independence to have contact and influence with other countries. It is not necessary now. Yet, many Americans have been led to believe that our country is so strong that it can defend, feed and subsidize half the world, while at the same time believing that we are so weak and "interdependent" that we cannot survive without pooling our resources and sovereignty with those we subsidize. If wanting no part of this kind of "logic" is isolationism, then it is time we brought it back into vogue.

Senator Robert A. Taft clearly explained our traditional foreign policy:

"Our traditional policy of neutrality and non-interference with other nations was based on the principle that this policy was the best way to avoid disputes with other nations and to maintain the liberty of this country without war. From the days of George Washington that has been the policy of the United States. It has never been isolationism; but it has always avoided alliances and interference in foreign quarrels as a preventive against possible war, and it has always opposed any commitment by the United States, in advance, to take any military action outside of our territory. It would leave us free to interfere or not according to whether we consider the case of sufficiently vital interest to the liberty of this country. It was the policy of the free hand." (A Foreign Policy for Americans, p. 12)

"But that is nationalism," chants the chorus. "And nationalism fosters jealousy, suspicion and hatred of other countries which in turn leads to war."[4] How many times has this utter nonsense been repeated without challenge as though it were some kind of empirical and self-evident truth! What kind of logic assumes that loving one's country means jealousy, suspicion and hatred of all others? Why can't we be proud of America as an independent nation and also have a feeling of brotherhood and respect for other peoples around the world? As a matter of fact, haven't Americans done just that for the past 200 years? What people have poured out more treasure to other lands, opened their doors to more immigrants, and sent more missionaries, teachers and doctors than we? Are we now to believe that love of our own country will suddenly cause us to hate the peoples of other lands?

It was the late Herbert Hoover who pointed out the social poison in the current derision of American nationalism:

"We must realize the vitality of the great spiritual force which we call nationalism. The fuzzy-minded intellectuals have sought to brand nationalism as a sin against mankind. They seem to think that infamy is attached to the word "nationalist." But that force cannot be obscured by denunciation of it as greed or selfishness—as it sometimes is. The spirit of nationalism springs from the deepest of human emotions. It rises from the yearning of men to be free of foreign domination, to govern themselves. It springs from a thousand rills of race, of history, of sacrifice and pride in national achievement." (Quoted by Eugene W. Castle, Billions, Blunders and Baloney, p. 259)

In order for a man to be a good neighbor within his own community, he had better first love his own family before he tries to save the neighborhood. If he doesn't love his own, why should we believe he would love others? Theodore Roosevelt firmly believed that "it is only the man who ardently loves his country first who in actual practice can help any other country at all." (P.P.N.S., p. 196)

Many well-intentioned people are now convinced that we are living in a period of history which makes it both possible and necessary to abandon our national sovereignty, to merge our nation militarily, economically, and politically with other nations, and to form, at last a world government which, supposedly, would put an end to war. We are told that this is merely doing between nations what we did so successfully with our thirteen colonies. This plea for world federalism is based on the idea that the mere act of joining separate political units together into a larger federal entity will somehow prevent those units from waging war with each other. The success of our own federal system is most often cited as proof that this theory is valid. But such an evaluation is a shallow one.

First of all, the American Civil War, one of the most bloody in all history, illustrates that the mere federation of governments, even those culturally similar, as in America, does not automatically prevent war between them. Secondly, we find that true peace quite easily exists between nations which are not federated. As a matter of fact, members of the British Commonwealth of Nations seemed to get along far more peacefully after the political bonds between them had been relaxed. In other words, true peace has absolutely nothing to do with whether separate political units are joined together – except, perhaps, that such a union may create a common military defense sufficiently impressive to deter an aggressive attack. But that is peace between the union and outside powers; it has little effect on peace between the units, themselves, which is the substance of the argument for world government.

Peace is the natural result of relationships between groups and cultures which are mutually satisfactory to both sides. These relationships are found with equal ease within or across federal lines. As a matter of fact, they are the relationships that promote peaceful conditions within the community and think for a moment; if you were marooned on an island with two other people, what relationships between you would be mutually satisfactory enough to prevent you from resorting to violence in your relationship? Or, to put it the other way around, what would cause you to break the peace and raise your hand against your partners?

Obviously, if one or both of the partners attempted to seize your food and shelter, you would fight. Their reaction to similar efforts on your part would be the same. If they attempted to take away your freedom, to dictate how you would conduct your affairs, or tell you what moral and ethical standards you must follow, likewise, you would fight. And if they constantly ridiculed your attire, your manners and your speech, in time you might be sparked into a brawl. The best way to keep the peace on that island is for each one to mind his own business, to respect each other's right to be different (even to act in a way that seems foolish or improper, if he wishes), and to have compassion for each other's troubles and hardships – but not to force each other to do something! And, to make sure that the others hold to their end of the bargain, each should keep physically strong enough to make any violation of this code unprofitable.[5]

Now, suppose these three got together and decided to form a political union, to "federate" as it were. Would this really change anything? Suppose they declared themselves to be the United Persons, and wrote a charter, and held daily meetings and passed resolutions. What then? These superficial ceremonies might be fun for awhile, but the minute two of them out-voted the other, and started "legally" to take his food and shelter, limit his freedom or force him to accept an unwanted standard of moral conduct, they would be right back where they all began. Federation or no federation, they would fight.

Is it really different between nations? Not at all. The same simple code of conduct applies in all human relationships, large or small. Regardless of the size, be it international or three men on an island, the basic unit is still the human personality. Ignore this fact, and any plan is doomed to failure.[6]

It might be worthwhile at this point to mention that Washington's policy of neutrality and non-interference was adhered to by those who followed him. For instance, President John Adams, in his Inaugural Address, resolved "to do justice as far as may depend upon me, at all times and to all nations, and maintain peace, friendship, and benevolence with all the world." He later said, in a special message to Congress:
"It is my sincere desire, and in this I presume I concur with you and with our constituents, to preserve peace and friendship with all nations..."

To which the Senate, presided over by Thomas Jefferson, replied:
"Peace and harmony with all nations is our sincere wish; but such being the lot of humanity that nations will not always reciprocate peaceable dispositions, it is our firm belief that effectual measures of defense will tend to inspire that national self-respect and confidence at home which is the unfailing source of respectability abroad, to check aggression and prevent war." (Quoted by Clarence B. Carson, The American Tradition, p. 210)

When the thirteen colonies formed our Federal Union, they had two very important factors in their favor, neither of which are present in the world at large today. First, the colonists themselves were all of a similar cultural background. They enjoyed similar legal systems, they spoke the same language, and they shared similar religious beliefs. They had much in common. The second advantage, and the most important of the two, was that they formed their union under a constitution which was designed to prevent any of them, or a majority of them, from forcefully intervening in the affairs of the others. The original federal government was authorized to provide mutual defense, run a post office, and that was about all. As previously mentioned, however, even though we had these powerful forces working in our favor, full scale war did break out at one tragic point in our history.

The peace that followed, of course, was no peace at all, but was only the smoldering resentment and hatred that follows in the wake of any armed conflict. Fortunately, the common ties between North and South, the cultural similarities and the common heritage, have proved through the intervening years to over-balance the differences. And with the gradual passing away of the generation that carried the battle scars, the Union has healed.

Among the nations of the world today, there are precious few common bonds that could help overcome the clash of cross-purposes that inevitably must arise between groups with such divergent ethnic, linguistic, legal, religious, cultural, and political environments. To add fuel to the fire, the concept woven into all of the present-day proposals for world government (The U.N. foremost among these) is one of unlimited governmental power to impose by force a monolithic set of values and conduct on all groups and individuals whether they like it or not. Far from insuring peace, such conditions can only enhance the chances of war.[7]

In this connection it is interesting to point out that the late J. Reuben Clark, who was recently described as "probably the greatest authority on [the Constitution] during the past fifty years" (American Opinion, April 1966, p. 113), in 1945 – the year the United Nations charter was adopted – made this prediction in his devastating and prophetic "cursory analysis" of the United Nations Charter:

"There seems no reason to doubt that such real approval as the Charter has among the people is based upon the belief that if the Charter is put into effect, wars will end. . . The Charter will not certainly end war. Some will ask – why not? In the first place, there is no provision in the Charter itself that contemplates ending war. It is true the Charter provides for force to bring peace, but such use of force is itself war. . . It is true the Charter is built to prepare for war, not to promote peace. . . The Charter is a war document, not a peace document.

"Not only does the Charter Organization not prevent future wars, but it makes it practically certain that we will have future wars, and as to such wars it takes from us the power to declare them, to choose the side on which we shall fight, to determine what forces and military equipment we shall use in the war, and to control and command our sons who do the fighting." (Unpublished Manuscript; quoted in P.P.N.S., p. 458)

Everyone is for peace and against war – particularly the horrors of nuclear war. And what are the horrors of war? Why, death, destruction and human suffering, of course! But, wait a minute. Since the big "peace" began at the end of World War II, isn't it a fact that, behind the iron and bamboo curtains, there has been more death, destruction and human suffering than in most of the big wars of history combined? Yes, it is a fact – a horrible fact – which Martin Dies, the former long-time Chairman of the House Committee on Un-American Activities, described in these words:

"In Russia, a minimum of 25,000,000 people have been starved to death and murdered in 45 years. In Red China, the figure is probably at least 35,000,000 in a short 12 years. These ruthless, inhuman atrocities have been investigated, documented and reported in print, by numerous committees of the Congress. Yet only a relative handful of Americans know where to look for the facts, or even know the reports exist; and still fewer have read them." (The Martin Dies Story, p. 20)

A consideration of these facts means that we have to redefine our terms when we talk about "peace." There are two kinds of peace. If we define peace as merely the absence of war, then we could be talking about the peace that reigns in a communist slave labor camp. The wretched souls in prison there are not at war, but do you think they would call it peace?

The only real peace – the one most of us think about when we use the term – is a peace with freedom. A Nation that is not willing, if necessary, to face the rigors of war to defend its real peace-in-freedom is doomed to lose both its freedom and its peace! These are the hard facts of life. We may not like them, but until we live in a far better world than exists today, we must face up to them squarely and courageously.[8]

In a discussion of war and its effects these wise words of James Madison should always be remembered:

"Of all the enemies to public liberty war is, perhaps, the most to be dreaded, because it comprises and develops the germ of every other. War is the parent of armies; from these proceed debts and taxes; and armies, and debts, and taxes are the known instruments for bringing the many under the domination of the few. In war, too, the discretionary power of the Executive is extended; its influence in dealing out offices, honors, and emoluments is multiplied; and all the means of seducing the minds, are added to those of subduing the force, of the people. The same malignant aspect in republicanism may be traced in the inequality of fortunes, and the opportunities of fraud, growing out of a state of war, and in the degeneracy of manners and of morals, engendered by both. No nation could preserve its freedom in the midst of continual warfare..." (April 20, 1795; Works 4:491–2; P.P.N.S., p. 468)

Shortly after this, in a letter to Thomas Jefferson, James Madison issued another warning which should never be forgotten:

"The management of foreign relations appears to be the most susceptible of abuse, of all the trusts committed to a Government, because they can be concealed or disclosed, or disclosed in such parts & at such times as will best suit particular views; and because the body of the people are less capable of judging and are more under the influence of prejudices, on that branch of their affairs, than of any other. Perhaps it is a universal truth that the loss of liberty at home is to be charged to provisions against danger real or pretended from abroad." (May 13, 1798; Works 2:140–1; P.P.N.S., p. 431)

Until all nations follow the concept of limited government, it is unlikely that universal peace will ever be realized on this planet. Unlimited, power-grasping governments will always resort to force if they think they can get away with it.[9] But there can be peace for America. As long as our leaders faithfully discharge their duty to preserve and strengthen the military, economic and political independence of our Republic, the world's petty despots will leave us alone. What more could we ask of U.S. foreign policy?

From these primary policy pronouncements some general principles emerge. They can be reduced to a few heads and stated as imperatives in the following manner:

The United States should:

Establish and maintain a position of independence with regard to other countries

Avoid political connection, involvement or intervention in the affairs of other countries

Make no permanent or entangling alliances

Treat all nations impartially, neither granting nor accepting special privileges from any

Promote commerce with all free peoples and countries

Cooperate with other countries to develop civilized rules of intercourse

Act always in accordance with the "laws of Nations"

Remedy all just claims of injury to other nations and require just treatment from other nations, standing ready, if necessary to punish offenders

Maintain a defensive force of sufficient magnitude to deter aggressors.[10] (See *The American Tradition*, p. 212)

For the first hundred years and more of the existence of the Republic, Americans developed and maintained a tradition that was in keeping with the above principles. We can say with confidence that the United States established a tradition of foreign relations in keeping with the principles laid down by the founding fathers. In the words of Senator Taft:

"I do not believe it a selfish goal for us to insist that the over-riding purpose of all American foreign policy should be the maintenance of the liberty and the peace of the people of the United States, so that they may achieve that intellectual and material improvement which is their genius and in which they can do an even greater service to mankind than we can by billions of material assistance – and more than we can ever do by war." (*A Foreign Policy For Americans*, p. 14)

It seems fitting in conclusion to refer you again to the inspired words of the wise father of our country. He said:

"My ardent desire is, and my aim has been. . . to keep the United States free from political connections with every other country, to see them independent of all and under the influence of none. In a word, I want an American character, that the powers of Europe may be convinced we act for ourselves, and not for others. This, in my judgment, is the only way to be respected abroad and happy at home." (October 9, 1795; Writings 13:119)

Endnotes

1. Address delivered on June 21, 1968, at the Farm Bureau Banquet in Preston, Idaho.

2. "Against the insidious wiles of foreign influence, I conjure you to believe me, my fellow–citizens, the jealousy of a free people ought to be constantly awake, since history and experience prove that foreign influence is one of the most baneful foes of republican Government.– But that jealousy, to be useful, must be impartial; else it becomes the instrument of the very influence to be avoided, instead of a defense against it." (President George Washington, Farewell Address, September 17, 1796; Writings 13:315)

3. "About to enter, fellow–citizens, on the exercise of duties which comprehend everything dear and valuable to you, it is proper you

should understand what I deem the essential principles of our Government, and consequently those which ought to shape its Administration. I will compress them within the narrowest compass they will bear, stating the general principle, but not all its limitations. Equal and exact justice to all men, of whatever state or persuasion, religious or political; peace, commerce, and honest friendship with all nations, entangling alliances with none; the support of the State governments in all their rights, as the most competent administrations for our domestic concerns and the surest bulwarks against anti-republican tendencies; the preservation of the General Government in its whole constitutional vigor, as the sheet anchor of our peace at home and safety abroad; a jealous care of the right of election by the people—a mild and safe corrective of abuses which are lopped by the sword of revolution where peaceable remedies are not provided; absolute acquiescence in the decisions of the majority, the vital principle of republics, from which is no appeal but to force, the vital principle and immediate parent of despotism; a well disciplined militia, our best reliance in peace and for the first moments of war, till regulars may relieve them; the supremacy of the civil over the military authority; economy in the public expense, that labor may be lightly burdened; the honest payment of our debts and sacred preservation of the public faith; encouragement of agriculture, and of commerce as its handmaid; the diffusion of information and arraignment of all abuses at the bar of the public reason; freedom of religion; freedom of the press, and freedom of person under the protection of the habeas corpus, and trial by juries impartially selected. These principles form the bright constellation which has gone before us and guided our steps through an age of revolution and reformation. The wisdom of our sages and blood of our heroes have been devoted to their attainment. They should be the creed of our political faith, the text of civic instruction, the touchstone by which to try the services of those we trust; and should we wander from them in moments of error or of alarm, let us hasten to retrace our steps and to regain the road which alone leads to peace, liberty, and safety. (Thomas Jefferson, First Inaugural Address, March 4, 1801; also known as the Creed of our Political Faith; Works 8:4–5)

4. Credit is given to G. Edward Griffin, The Fearful Master, for some of the thoughts expressed in this chapter.

5. "It takes a combination of three factors to protect our national interests under all conditions and to maintain peace on our terms. The three factors are: credible military superiority along the entire spectrum of modern warfare; courageous and decisive diplomacy; and the active support of the American people." (General Thomas S. Power, Design for Survival, p. 6)

6. "Those who have written on civil government lay it down as a first principle, and all historians demonstrate the same, that whoever would found a state and make proper laws for the government of it must presume that all men are bad by nature: that they will not fail to show that natural depravity of heart whenever they have a fair opportunity. . . constant experience shows us that every man vested with power is apt to abuse it. He pushes on till he comes to something that limits him." (Machiavelli, 1469–1527; quoted by John Adams, Works 4:408)

7. "Power and law are not synonymous. In truth they are frequently in opposition and irreconcilable. There is God's Law from which all Equitable laws of man emerge and by which men must live if they are not to die in oppression, chaos and despair. Divorced from God's eternal and immutable Law, established before the founding of the suns, man's power is evil no matter the noble words with which it is employed or the motives urged when enforcing it. Men of good will, mindful therefore of the Law laid down by God, will oppose governments whose rule is by men, and if they wish to survive as a nation they will destroy the government which attempts to adjudicate by the whim of venal judges." (Cicero, quoted in A Pillar of Iron, p. ix)

8. "It is our duty. . . to endeavor to avoid war; but if it shall actually take place, no matter by whom brought on, we must defend ourselves. If our house be on fire, without inquiring whether it was fired from

within or without, we must try to extinguish it." (Thomas Jefferson, to James Lewis, May 9, 1798; Works 4:241)

9. "There is one safeguard known generally to the wise, which is an advantage and security to all, but especially to democracies as against despots. What is it? Distrust." (Demosthenes, 384–322 B.C.; Familiar Quotations, p. 277)

10. "Deterrence is more than bombs and missiles and tanks and armies. Deterrence is a sound economy and prosperous industry. Deterrence is scientific progress and good schools. Deterrence is effective civil defense and the maintenance of law and order. Deterrence is the practice of religion and respect for the rights and convictions of others. Deterrence is a high standard of morals and wholesome family life. Deterrence is honesty in public office and freedom of the press. Deterrence is all these things and many more, for only a nation that is healthy and strong in every respect has the power and will to deter the forces from within and without that threaten its survival." (General Thomas S. Power, Design for Survival, p. 242)

FREEDOM AND FREE ENTERPRISE

My soul is subdued and my feeling a bit tender as I look into your faces tonight. I speak to you humbly and gratefully. I am not here to tickle your ears or entertain you. I shall speak to you honestly and frankly. The message I bring is not a particularly happy one. But it is the truth and time is on the side of truth. I love this county with all my heart I love America. I have traveled abroad just enough and returned to the shores of this land scores of times to make me appreciate deeply what we have here. And as I return, I often think of the words of Scott when he said:

Breathes there the man with soul so dead
Who never to himself hath said,
This is my own, my native land!
Whose heart hath ne'er within him burn'd
As home his footsteps he hath turn'd
From wandering on a foreign strand?
If such there breathe, go, mark him well!
(Sir Walter Scott, 1771–1832, Lay of the Last Minstrel. Canto vi. Stanza 1)

...and so on. Sometimes I think of the words of Van Dyke in that great poem, "America for Me", part of which goes:

'Tis fine to see the Old World, and travel up and down
Among the famous palaces and cities of renown,

To admire the crumbly castles and the statues of the kings

But now I think I've had enough of antiquated things… Oh, it's home again, and home again, America for me!

I want a ship that's westward bound to plough the rolling sea,

In the land of youth and freedom beyond the ocean bars,

Where the air is full of sunlight and the flag is full of stars!

And so tonight, I appreciate more than I can say this opportunity to speak to you frankly as an American; one who prizes his citizenship in this blessed land. It seems appropriate that I should say a few words in regards to freedom and liberty. It is by vigilance by business people such as you represent who rely on our great inspired free enterprise system that our liberties will be maintained.

However, far too many today are enjoying a comfortable complacency. As a lead into my message I quote from my friend, Dean Clarence Manion in the Manion Forum Bulletin of July 3, 1977. He said in these days of pompous highbrowed drivel about the establishment of human rights throughout the world it is most encouraging to find two distinguished university professors publishing jointly the following fact of history. Listen to it:

"Humanity has survived in various states of tyranny for thousands of years. One might even say that this is the natural state of affairs for man. Future historians may look back and see the period 1776–1976 as a brief 200 year accident."

I don't believe it's an accident in the history of man in which real freedom existed for all. Yes, we are a prosperous nation, our people have high paying jobs, our incomes are high, our standard of living is at an unprecedented level. We do not like to be disturbed as we enjoy our life of ease. We live in the soft present and feel the future is secure. We do not worry about history. We seem oblivious to the causes to the rises and falls of nations. We are blind to the hard fact that nations usually sow the seeds of their own destruction while enjoying unprecedented prosperity. I say to you with all the fervor of my soul, we are sowing the seeds of our own destruction in America and much of the free world today.

It is my sober warning to you today that if the trends of the past forty years and especially the last fifteen years continue we will lose that which is as priceless as life itself: our freedom, our liberty, our right to act as free men. It can happen here, it is happening here. The outlook for free enterprise in the world has never seemed so uncertain as now.

Nationalization is growing rapidly especially outside of the Western Hemisphere. Many nations have a mixed economy brought about by an increase in state control and a corresponding weakening of the private enterprise system. In our own county we unmistakably see a trend toward welfare-statism, what one has called pension fund socialism. It seems in vogue for some to raise the question, will capitalism survive? More appropriately the question might be stated; Do we as American citizens have the desire and will for capitalism, and free enterprise to survive?

Today it seems evident that we are rearing a generation of Americans who do not understand the productive base of our society and how we came by such prosperity. Evidence of this fact is found in surveys taken among some of our high school and college students. The majority of whom it is reported believe private enterprise is a failure. Although they don't have a clear understanding of what private enterprise is. With them as with many adults there is a vague notion that it is some unfair system which stands to give special advantage to big corporations and wealthy individuals. From a study done by the council of economic education, in 1973, 50% of the high school students could not distinguish between collectivism and a free enterprise society. 50% did not know the United States economy was based on free enterprise. From another study done by the Opinion Research Corporation, the median estimate of the U.S. public was that corporation profits are 28% of the sales dollar. Actually profits are 4 or 5%. These attitudes may be the result of the propaganda by certain textbook writers who hold the idea in many instances that a planned economy is the remedy for all of our economic ills and weakness in our American way of life, to which they readily point without referring to the magnificent fruits of the system.

Before a welfare state can flourish, a welfare state mentality must have taken root. Are we not today yielding the harvest of seeds sown from the days of the great depression to the present? The ethic of the day seems calculated to indoctrinate our citizens for a dependency on the state. Our founding fathers recognized that certain rights are inalienable, that is, God given. Today the state is looked to as the guarantor of human rights, life, liberty and property. Our forbearers practiced the biblical ethic that man should earn his bread by the sweat of his own brow. Today's ethic seems to be that it is right to be supported by the sweat of another's brow.

Tonight may I state the case for the free market and how it operates? You folks know already pretty well how it operates. I would also emphasize why a free market is essential to regaining political and economic freedoms. The more I become acquainted with the appalling lack of understanding of our free market system, the more I become convinced that we must return to something of a basic primer to explain our economic system. Perhaps this parable will illustrate.

Two fathers lived side by side as neighbors. Each had two sons. Both fathers had good jobs, roomy homes and material means to provide the best of life's luxuries. The essential difference between the two fathers was one of philosophy. Mr. A's objective with his two sons was to instill principles that would bring about self respect, personal responsibility and independence. His methods narrowed our scrutiny. When his boys were young he taught them how to work, that of simple tasks by his side. When they became more mature he developed a work incentive program. The pay scale was commensurate to the quality of work performed. An average job for example paid 50 cents, above average 60, and exceptional job, 75. A one dollar job the impossible task a goal that he soon observed his boys were striving after. He impressed on his sons that the only limit on the earning were their personal initiative and desire. He emphasized that necessity to postpone immediate wants so they could save for the future. The lessons were well learned over a period of time. There was an under girding moral element to Mr. A's philosophy. A principle more caught than taught. A simple example will suffice. One day the boys, now young men were working in Mr. A's plant. He observed some sloppy work being done on one of the products. He asked to see the products and proceeded to remove the name plate. One of the boys resisted, "Why are you doing that dad?" Mr. A replied, "I'll not have my name attached to a shoddy product. When my name goes on, my customers must know I've given them my best workmanship. Would you want to own this product?" It was an answer which provided a lesson that would last a lifetime. How could the golden rule be emphasized more effectively in business?

Mr. B also had a philosophy, albeit a reactionary one to his early struggles of youth. I'll not have my kids go through what I did. His philosophy was to remove the struggle from life. His method also merits our consideration. Regularly his sons were provided with generous allowances. Little work in their formative years was expected. In later years the boys were encouraged to work, but were now too comfortable in their security. After all they had all of their material wants satisfied. At this junction Mr. B made a profound discovery: wants always exceed basic needs and are never satisfied unless disciplined. To counteract the lack of self discipline Mr. B. embarked on a routine of imposed restraints. To his chagrin, he found his boys embittered toward him, ungrateful and frequently disobedient to the rules imposed on them. Need I draw the conclusions from this parable? Is it not apparent which philosophy leads to a productive, contributive member of society and which philosophy sponsors dependency? Is it also not apparent which philosophy will best prepare one for an emotional or economic crisis? I do not apologize for the simplicity of the illustration. One may argue the characters are exaggerated. But even a child can understand the effect of Mr. B's care taker philosophy. Is not this philosophy analogous in many ways to the government official who argues, "in this county welfare is no longer charity, it is a right." More and more Americans feel that the government owes them something. But it is not Mr. B's philosophy that commands our attention tonight, it is Mr. A's. Why is it the elements in his philosophy are so unfamiliar to so many that they believe that their government owes them something? Our task is to make Mr. A's philosophy both familiar and credible. When it is understood and believed, it will be defended with the same determination and vigor that our founding fathers pledged their lives, their fortunes and their sacred honor. Many of you see the idea of the free enterprise or the free market system as only an alternative economic system to our other systems. This is a serious oversight and causes many to miss the most crucial element to the free market system. May I mention some of these features?

1. The free market system rests on a moral base.

Before one can appreciate why this premise is true, two questions must be answered:

First, what is man?

The second question, a corollary to the first, is from what source does man derive his rights?

Our governmental system like ancient Israel and biblical Christianity recognized man as a special creature of God, a special creation of God. He is not as some theorists reason, a product of chance or merely an educated animal. His paternal origin comes from God. Thus man inherently possesses God implanted attributes and potential: reason, free agency, judgment, compassion, initiative, and a personal striving for perfection.

From what source does man derive his rights? There can be only two possible origins of man's rights; rights are either God given as part of the divine plan or they are granted by government as part of the political plan. Reason, necessity, tradition and religious convictions all led the founding fathers of this republic to accept the divine origin of these rights. If we accept the premise that human rights are granted by government, then we must be willing to accept the corollary that they can be denied by government. I for one shall never accept that premise. As the French political economist, Frederick Bastiat phrased it so succinctly. "Life, liberty and property do not exist because men have made laws. On the contrary, it was the fact that life, liberty and property existed beforehand that caused man to make laws in the first place."

Since God created man with certain inalienable rights and man in turn created government to help secure and safeguard those rights, it follows that man is superior to government and should remain master over it, not the other way around. Even the non-believer can appreciate the logic of this relationship. Thus we see that the principle of supremacy of the individual over government is rooted in religious precept. This is why the founders of our nations were so influenced by the writings of John Locke, which declared that man was naturally in a state of perfect freedom, that he had a right to preservation and property, and that the source of all this was God.

The founding fathers recognized that no people can maintain freedom unless their political institutions are founded on faith in God and belief in the existence of moral law. They realized that to survive, this new nation needed a reliance on the protection of God. In the Declaration of Independence we find their appeal to the supreme judge of the world and to the laws of nature and nature's God. The document includes their acclamation of a firm reliance on the protection of divine providence. The implication of this moral basis to our political economic system is that God is the dispenser of mans rights not government. The inalienable right of free choice is implanted in the human breast. Man is born to choose for himself. This is why man cannot be driven indefinitely or led by despotic leaders to intellectual, physical or economic bondage. Fear and despotism may rule for a generation, two or three, but in time the human spirit rebels. The spirit of liberty manifests itself and the tyrannical hand of despotism is overthrown. May it ever be so.

Once a person awakens to the truth of his divine identity he demands his rights, the right to property, the right to make his own decisions, the right to plan his own welfare, the right to improve himself materially, intellectually and spiritually.

2. The free market is based on the right to property.

The right to property is again based on a scriptural precept. It recognizes that the earth belongs to the Lord, that He created it for man's blessing and benefit. Thus man's desire to own property, his own home and goods, his own business is desirable and good. Utopian and communitarian schemes which eliminate property rights are not only unworkable, they deny to man his inherent desire to improve his station. They are therefore contrary to the pursuit of happiness. With no property rights, man's incentive would be diminished to satisfying only his barest necessities such as food and clothing. How this truth is evident in the communist countries today! No property rights, no incentive to individual enterprise to risk one's own capital because the fruits of ones labor could not be enjoyed. No property rights, no contractual relationship to buy and sell because title to possession of goods could not be granted. No property rights, no recognition of divine law which prohibits man from stealing and coveting others' possessions; one cannot steal that which belongs to everyone, nor can he covet that which is not another's. No property rights, no possibility of the sanctity of ones own home and the joy which come from creation, production and ownership.

A free market society recognizes private property as sacred because the individual is entitled to ownership of goods and property which he has earned; he is sovereign so far as human law is concerned over his own goods. He may retain possession of his goods; he may pass his wealth on to his family or to charitable causes. For one cannot give what one does not own.

James Madison recognized that property consisted not only of man's external goods, his land, merchandise and money, but more sacredly he had title to his thoughts, opinions, and conscience. The civil government's obligation then is to safeguard this right and to frame laws which secure to every man the free exercise of his conscience and the right and control of his property. No liberty is possible except a man is protected in his title to his legal holdings and property and can be indemnified by the law for its loss or destruction. Remove this right and man is reduced to serfdom.

Former United States Supreme Court Justice George Southerland said it this way: "To give man liberty but take from him the property which is the fruit and badge of his liberty is to still leave him a slave."

3. The free market is based on the right to enjoy private enterprise for profit.

As a country we have suffered under half a century of liberal propaganda demeaning economic success. This was done by referring to men who are willing to risk their capital, their profit in tools and equipment, as coupon clippers, economic royalists, capitalists, and profiteers, as though there were something inherently evil in profit.

Profit is the reward for honest labor. It is the incentive that causes a man to risk his capital to build a business. If he cannot keep or invest that which he has earned, neither may he own, nor will he risk. Profit creates wealth. Wealth creates more work opportunities. And more work opportunities creates greater wealth. None of this is possible without incentive. There is another benefit to profit. It provides man with moral choices. With profit man can choose to be greedy and selfish, he can invest and expand thereby providing others with jobs, he can be charitable. Charity is not charity unless it is voluntary. It cannot be voluntary if there is nothing to give. Only safe profit creates more jobs, not government. The only way government can create jobs is to take the money from productive citizens in the form of taxes and transfer it to government programs. Without someone generating profit which can be taxed, government revenue is not possible.

4. The free market is the right to voluntary exchange of goods and services, free from restraints and controls.

Nothing is more to be prized, nor more sacred than man's free choice. Free choice is the essence of free enterprise. It recognizes that the common man will make choices in his own self interest. It allows the manufacturer to produce what he wants, how much, and to set his own price. It allows the buyer to decide if he wants a certain product at the price established. It preserves the right to work when and where we choose. In his first inaugural address, Thomas Jefferson said that, "the sum of good government shall leave citizens free to regulate their own pursuits of industry and improvement and shall not take from the mouth of labor the bread it has earned."

Why does our system produce more bread, manufacture more shoes and assemble more TV sets than Russian socialism? It does so precisely because our government does not guarantee these things; if it did there would be so many accompanying taxes, controls, regulations and political manipulations that the productive genius based on freedom of choice that is Americas would soon be reduced to the floundering level of waste and inefficiency now found behind the Iron Curtain.

When government presumes to demand more and more of the fruits of a man's labor through taxation and reduces more and more his actual income by printing money and furthering debt, the wage earner is left with less and less to buy food, to provide housing, medical care, education and private welfare. The individuals are left without a choice and must look to the state as its benevolent supporter of these services. When that happens liberty is gone.

5. A free market survives with competition.

Were it not for competition among goods and services, there would be no standard by which a buyer could discern shoddy merchandise or inept service from excellence. Were it not for competition, the seller could price his goods and services according to his own fancy. It is competition that determines what is good, better, and best. It is competition that determines the price for products or services. If goods are overpriced in comparison with other comparable goods, the buyer refuses to buy, thus forcing the seller to drop his price. There is a glaring paradox in our society; in the one hand legislation has been enacted to allegedly prevent one business or combination of businesses, monopolies, from disrupting or eliminating competitors in the market; on the other hand we have yet to fully awaken to the worst form of monopolistic practice currently impeding the free market. I refer to government monopoly.

When government, by either ownership or regulation, prevents the full freedom of action by sellers, this of course regulates and controls prices. No better example exists today than the so called energy crisis. As a nation we have artificially regulated the price of natural gas for over 20 years. The Federal Power Commission has set prices and burdened the oil industry with regulations. Consequently the oil industry has not had the incentive to discover natural gas or drill for oil even though the reserves are there. The environmentalists, with the help of activist lawyers, have combined to make it almost impossible to drill for oil economically. What industry wants to risk its capital fighting through the hearings and lawsuits which double and triple its investment costs? So exploration does not take place. Our reserves are kept off the market to await the day when government will deregulate. The most effective energy policy our government could devise would be to step out of the regulatory business. This would provide, once again, the incentives for industry to make investment and make exploration. Freedom from bureaucratic monopoly is essential to allow our free market to work properly. I hope we wake up to this serious lesson before our freedoms are lost altogether.

We have talked so far about the vital elements to a free market operation. How does it all work together to bring about needed goods and services? Let me illustrate. There could be many illustrations. How do our cities and towns each day obtain the quantity of food products they demand? Of all agencies engaged in supplying cities with food almost no one knows how much the city consumes or how much is being produced. Despite this ignorance the cities receive about the amount of food needed without great service or shortage. How is this accomplished without a central directing body telling each producer what it should produce?

The answer of course is the operation of the free market, free enterprise in action. Suppose, for example, that a given city did not receive the amount for food products needed to satisfy its demand. Rather than go without, many people would be willing to pay higher prices. Thus prices would increase and the volume of production would rise, or the volume flowing to that city would increase. This would end the shortage. More food would be shipped to this city and less to other places. Or suppose there was an oversupply of food products. To avoid spoilage the seller would lower his price; this in turn is a signal to a producer to cut back on production. Thus the over supply is automatically regulated. Less food is shipped to that city and more to other cities. No bureau in all of Washington could perform this service. It has been tried and failed in many industries. Just as price regulates the distribution of food in a given city, so it also determines the total amount produced in the country. Greater profits provide farmers with the incentive to produce a greater product. If the supply increased at a pace faster than a demand for a product, farmers and ranchers are compelled to lower their prices.

As it becomes less profitable to produce potential producers, marginal producers are deterred from engaging in this occupation and the unprofitable producers divert to something else or abandon farming altogether. This is how this remarkable system works. This is how it has built this nation as the strongest nation in the world. Yes, this is how it works in all industries when government controls and planning controls and price fixing are left out. Yet few of our citizens seem to understand this. Economic literacy among our people has not been one of the bright spots in our 200 year old history. Yet it is apparent that when ignorance prevails the people eventually suffer. The principles behind our American free market economy can be reduced to a rather simple formula. Here it is, and I hope if you forget everything else I said, you'll remember this formula. It is so basic and so simple.

Free Market Economy's Simple Formula

1. Economic security for all is impossible without widespread abundance.

2. Abundance is impossible without industrious and ambitious production.

3. Such production is impossible without energetic, willing and eager labor.

4. This labor is not possible without incentive.

5. Of all forms of incentive, the freedom to obtain a reward for ones labors is the most sustaining for most people, sometimes called the "profit motive". It is simply the right to plan and to earn, and to enjoy the fruits of your labor.

6. This profit motive diminishes as government controls, regulations and taxes increase to deny the fruits of success to those who produce.

7. Therefore any attempt through government intervention to redistribute the material rewards of labor can only result in the eventual destruction of the productive base of society, without which real

abundance and security for more than the ruling elite is quite impossible.

Yes, what worked for Mr. A. in producing self disciplined, responsible, contributive sons to society works for a community. What works for a community will work for a state and what works for a state will work for this nation if we as American citizens demand that government officials perform only those duties provided by the Constitution and the Bill of Rights.

The Constitutions of the United States, an inspired document, is a solemn agreement between the citizens of this nation that every officer of this government is under a sacred duty to obey. The Constitution provides that the great bulk of legitimate activities of government are to be carried out at the state or local level. This is the only way in which the principle of self government can be made effective and safeguarded.

The smallest or lowest level that can possibly undertake the task is the one that should do so. The smaller the government unit and the closer it is to the people, the easier it is to guide it, to correct it, to keep it solvent and to keep our freedom. A category of government activity that poses the greatest danger to our continued freedom is the activity not within the proper sphere of government. The Constitution provides the federal government with no authority to grant such powers as welfare programs, schemes for redistributing the wealth and activities that coerce people into acting in accordance with a proscribed code of social planning.

There is one simple test to the constitutionality of a principle, do I as an individual have the right to use force upon my neighbor to accomplish this goal? If I do then I may delegate that power to my government to exercise it in my behalf. If I do not have that right, I can not delegate it. If we permit government to manufacture its own authority and to create self proclaimed powers not delegated to it by the people then the creature exceeds the creator and becomes master. Who is to say this far but no farther? What clear principle will stay the hand of government from reaching farther and farther into our daily lives?

Grover Cleveland said, "That though the people support the government, the government should not support the people." Once government steps over this clear line between the protective or negative role into the aggressive role of redistributing the wealth through taxation and providing so called benefits for some of its citizens it becomes a means for legalized plunder. Examples abound in the world of the failure of alternative systems to the free market.

What amazes me is that we cannot see from their example the obvious failure of socialism, what is does to a nation's economy, and how it morally debilitates a people. Great Britain is a tragic example of this. I was there just a short time ago. Here's a nation which I love, and here is a nation which has provided the free world with a tradition of freedom and democratic rights stemming from Magna Carta and coming down through other historical documents and statements through famous Englishmen, yet even today is losing her freedom. She has become a giant welfare state. Today government spending in Brittan amounts to 60% of her total national income. This is socialism. Medical doctors under socialized medicine are leaving Great Brittan in record numbers as are thousands of others. British Prime Minister James Callaghan in a speech last September said, "we used to think that you could just spend your way out of a recession and increase employment by cutting taxes and boosting government spending. I tell you in all candor that that option no longer exists and that in so far as it ever did exist, it only worked by injecting bigger doses of inflation into the economy, followed by higher levels of unemployment as the next step. That is the history of the past 20 years."

Such confession has led the renowned economist, Dr. Milton Friedman, to comment, "That must surely rank as one of the most remarkable and courageous statements ever made by a leader of a democratic government. I'll read it again. Savor it. "It is a confession of the intellectual bankruptcy, of the policy that has guided every British government in the post–war period, not only labor governments, but also Tory governments, of the policy that has guided almost every other western government, including the United States, under both

Republican and Democratic administrations, of the policy that is now being recommended to Mr. Carter by his advisors."

Consider another example, our neighbor to the north, Canada. For 20 years, 1944 to 1964, Saskatchewan, Canada lived under a socialist government. Here is what their Premiere, the honorable W. Ross Thatcher, said about this experience: "In 1944, the socialists said they would solve the unemployment problems by building government factories. They promised to use the profits to build highways, schools, hospitals, and to finance better social welfare measures generally. Over the years they set up 22 so-called crown or government corporations. By the time we had taken over at the end of the 20 year period, 12 of the crown corporations had gone bankrupt or been disposed of; others were kept operating by repeated and substantial government grants.

During the whole period, the socialists waged war against private business. The making of profits was condemned as an unforgivable sin. What was the result? Investors simply turned their back on the socialists. Dozens of oil companies pulled up stakes and moved out. Gas exploration ground to a complete halt. Prospecting in our vast north became almost nonexistent. During the period, Canada was experiencing the greatest economic boom in her history. Saskatchewan received only a handful of new factories.

After 18 years of socialism, there were fewer jobs in manufacturing than existed in 1945, this despite the investment of 500 million dollars, in crown corporations. During the period, more than 600 completely new taxes were introduced; 650 other taxes were increased. Per capita taxes in Saskatchewan were soon substantially out of line with our sister provinces; one more reason why industry located elsewhere. The socialists promised to make Saskatchewan a Mecca for the working man. Instead, we saw the greatest mass exodus of people out of an area since Moses lead the Jews out of Egypt, since the lower of 270,000 of our citizens left Saskatchewan to find employment elsewhere. If there are any Americans who think socialism is the answer, I wish they would come to Saskatchewan to study what has happened to our province."

We say it can't happen here. The lesson of New York City should tell us this same thing is happening here to us, now. As Dr. Friedman has pointed out, "New York City is no longer governed by its elected officials; it is governed by a committee of overseers appointed by the state of New York. New York City has partially lost its freedom."

When will we learn the lesson that fiscal irresponsibility leads to a loss of self government? When will we learn that when you lose economic independence, you lose political freedom? We have accepted a frightening degree of socialism in our country; the question is how much? The amount of freedom depends upon the amount of federal control in spending. A good measurement is to determine the amount or percentage of income of the people which is taken over and spent by the state. In Russia, the individual works almost wholly for the state leaving little for his own welfare. Scandinavia takes about 65–70% of the increase of the people; England some 60%. The United States is now approximately 44%.

America was built on the principle of faith in God, self reliance, the profit motive, individual action and voluntary charity. It was built by those who believed the surest helping hand was at the end of their own sleeves. These forefathers of ours shared one thing in common: an unshakable faith in God and a faith in themselves. There are indications that America is moving away from the philosophy that made her the most prosperous nation in the world.

In effect we are moving toward the philanthropic philosophy of Mr. B and abandoning the work incentive philosophy of Mr. A. Mr. B's philosophy has crept in unawares under the guise of a new name, egalitarianism. It is of course the socialist doctrine of equality. It struck a sympathetic chord with most Americans because its initial goal was equality of rights. Today, however, the goal for the proponents of equality is to restructure our entire economic system, using the power of the federal government to enforce their grand design. They now advocate throughout our economy that they redistribute wealth and income, a good definition of socialism. Our present middle of the road policy is as Von Mises – whom I class as the greatest economist that we have ever known – suggested: "socialism by the installment plan."

Americans have always been committed to taking care of the poor, aged, and unemployed. We've done this on the basis of Judaic Christian beliefs and humanitarian principles. It has been fundamental to our way of life that charity is to be voluntary if it is to be charity. Compulsory benevolence is not charity. Today's egalitarians are using the federal government to redistribute wealth in our society, not as a matter of voluntary charity, but as a matter of right. The chief weapon used by the federal government to achieve this equality is through so called transfer payments. This is a term which simply means that the federal government collects from one income group and transfers payments to another by their tax system. These payments are made in the forms of social security benefits, housing subsidies, Medicare, food stamps, to name a few. Today, total cost of such programs will exceed one hundred and fifty billion dollars annually. That represents about 44% of the total of all government federal spending, or about one dollar out of every seven of personal income.

When will we resolve as Americans that a dollar cannot make the trip to Washington D.C. and back without a bureaucratic bite being taken out of it? Medicaid, the government's regular health program for the poor, cost tax payers thirteen billion in '75. Medicare, the program for the disabled and elderly cost fifteen billion. Aid to families with dependent children cost over five billion. And about three billion is spent on food stamps. This is to name only a few of the so called benefits paid out. Our present social security program has been going in the hole at a rate of twelve billion dollars a year and yet the party now in power wants to increase the benefits to include a comprehensive national health insurance program. Recognizing that the present program will be insolvent by 1985, President Carter has now recommended that social security be funded out of a general income tax fund. Charges are made in the last election campaign that the social security program was going bankrupt. These charges were denied. Now the truth is out. The President's recommendation must be regarded as an admission of the failure of the present system and as a calculated policy to take this country into full scale socialism.

Our major danger is that we are currently and have been for forty years transferring responsibility from local and state governments to the federal government, precisely the same course which led to the economic collapse of Great Britain and New York. We cannot long pursue this present trend without it bringing us to national insolvency. Edmund Burke, a great British political philosopher warned of the threat of egalitarianism, socialism. He said, "A perfect equality will indeed be produced. That is to say equal wretchedness, equal beggary, and on the part of the petitioners, a woeful, helpless, and desperate disappointment, such is the event of all compulsory equalizations. They pull down what is above, they never raise what is below and they depress high and low together beneath the level of what was originally the lowest." All would like to be equalized with those who are better off than themselves, I suppose. They fail to realize that income is different and will always differ because people differ in their economic drive and ability.

History indicates that governments have been unable to prevent inequality of incomes. Further equalization efforts stifle initiative and retard progress to the extent that the real incomes of everyone are lower. We must remember that government assistance and control are essentially political provisions, and that experience has demonstrated that for that reason, they are not sufficiently stable to warrant their utilization as a foundation for sound economic growth under a free economic system.

The best way - the American way - is still maximum freedom for the individual guaranteed by a wise government that provides for the police department and national defense. History records that eventually people get the form of government they deserve. Good government which guarantees the maximum of freedom, liberty, and devolvement of the individual must be based upon sound principles. We must ever remember that ideas and principles are either sound or unsound in spite of those who hold them. Freedom of achievement has produced and will continue to produce the maximum of benefits in terms of human welfare.

Freedom is an eternal principle. Heaven disapproves of force, coercion and intimidation. Only a free people can be truly a happy people.

Of all sad things in the world, the saddest in the world is to see the people who have once known liberty and freedom and then lost it. I have seen the unquenchable yearning of the human heart for liberty. On an unforgettable occasion, yes on several occasions, this particular experience is indelibly etched on the memory of my soul. I saw this yearning spirit in the faces of many European people in the aftermath of World War II. It fell my lot, as President under the direction of the church, to be among the first to go without my family into war torn European countries and distribute food, clothing, and bedding to the suffering members of our church and others.

I saw during that year long visit first hand entire nation's prospect, flat on their backs economically. I looked into the face of hunger, the pale within, the many dressed in rags and some are foot. I saw the poor refugees, the poor unwanted souls who were driven from their homes to destinations unknown. They came with all their earthly possessions on their backs. I visited some of their homes, shacks, where as many as twenty two people were living in one room, four complete families. I saw many enslaved by habit barter their scanty ration of food and clothing for a cigarette. I saw some fortunate to get hold of an American magazine and pour over its pages and wonder if what they saw could possibly be true. I saw once happy freedom loving people in bondage under godless leadership. I saw the struggle on every hand to get to America, some legal and others illegal, all in an effort to enjoy freedom and liberty. These were the people, many of them who had once known some freedom, but had lost it.

Yes, we are a prosperous people today because of a political, economic system founded on spiritual values, not material values alone. It is founded on freedom of choice, free agency and eternal God given principles, and personal virtue. The Founding Fathers, though inspired they were, did not invent the priceless blessings of individual freedom and respect for the dignity of man; no, that priceless gift to mankind sprang from the God of heaven and not from government. Recognizing this truth, they forged the safeguards that would bind men's lust for power to the Constitution. They recognized that freedom must be perpetually preserved to be enjoyed. Each new generation must learn that truth anew. Yes, America's foundation is spiritual. Without the moral base to our system, we are no better off than any other nations which are now sunk into oblivion.

There are some in this land - among whom I count myself - whose faith it is that this land is reserved for only a righteous people and we remain here as tenants only as we remain in the favor of the Lord. And he is the landlord as far as this earth is concerned. If we are to remain under heaven's protection and care, we must return to those principles which have brought us our peace, liberty and prosperity. Our problems today are essentially problems of the spirit. "We here in America," as Theodore Roosevelt said over a half century ago, "hold in our hands the hope of the world, the fate of the coming years and shame and disgrace will be ours if, in our eyes the light of higher resolve is dimmed, if we trail in the dust of golden hopes of men."

You who gathered here tonight are dedicated to maintain that light of high resolve in the American people. As you do so, may I leave with you this challenge that you help others see that the real issue is not over economic systems, it is the issue of freedom and limited or no freedom, the same issue that brought about this nation's birth and independence.

Yes, with God's help and inspiration perhaps we may rekindle a flame of liberty that will last us long as time endures. For this I pray and thank you for this opportunity of meeting with you tonight.

OUR IMMEDIATE RESPONSIBILITY

Because of the nature of the message I bring to you, I have committed most of it to writing. I shall speak to you frankly and honestly. What I shall say are my personal convictions born out of an active life which has taken me into some forty-five nations and brought me close to the insidious forces that would destroy our way of life in this choice land. I express these convictions and warnings today because of my love for you and our beloved country.

A Message of Warning
The message I bring is not a happy one, but it is the truth – and time is always on the side of truth. I take as my theme the words of President David O. McKay, God's mouthpiece on the earth today, a Prophet of God:

"The position of this church on the subject of communism has never changed. We consider it the greatest satanical threat to peace, prosperity and the spread of God's work among men that exists on the face of this earth." (Conference Report, April, 1966, p. 109.)

"No greater immediate responsibility rests upon the members of the church, upon all citizens of this republic and of neighboring republics than to protect the freedom vouchsafed by the Constitution of the United States." (The Instructor, August, 1953)

In the days of the Prophet Noah, men had no greater immediate responsibility than to repent and board the Ark. Now in our day, the day of the Prophet David O. McKay, he has said that we have no greater immediate responsibility than to protect the freedom vouchsafed by the Constitution of the United States.

At the last general conference of the church (October 1966), President McKay, in his opening address, said:

"Efforts are being made to deprive man of his free agency – to steal from the individual his liberty.... There has been an alarming increase in the abandoning of the ideals that constitute the foundation of the Constitution of the United States."

Toward the close of his talk, our Prophet, quoting Paul's letter to Timothy regarding the preaching of the word, said:

"There should be no question in the mind of any true latter day saint as to what we shall preach... the gospel plan of salvation."

Then President McKay lists the areas our preaching should cover and admonishes us to include in our preaching what governments should or should not do in the interests of the preservation of our freedom.

Discourses on Freedom

Do we preach what governments should or should not do as a part of the gospel plan, as President McKay has urged or do we refuse to follow the Prophet by preaching a limited gospel plan of salvation? The fight for freedom cannot be divorced from the gospel – the plan of salvation.

We sing that we are thankful to "God for a Prophet to guide us in these latter days." By commandment of the Lord we assemble in general conference twice a year to get that guidance from the Lord's representative. Do we realize that in the last five years prior to October Conference, the Prophet has key noted three of these conferences with an opening discourse on freedom and given nine other addresses in the conferences that touched on freedom?

Do we see any pattern here? Can we name any other gospel theme that has received as much emphases from the man who holds the keys as has the theme of freedom?

We do not need a prophet – we have one. What we need is a listening ear, a humble heart, and a soul that is pure enough to follow his inspired guidance.

Now why this consistent voice of warning from the Prophet?

Statistics on Communism

Consider the following: Since World War II the Communists have brought under bondage – enslaved – on the average approximately 6,000 persons per hour, 144,000 per day, 52,000,000 per year – every hour of every day of every year since 1945.

Since 1945 the Communists have murdered in one country alone enough people to wipe out the entire population of over fifteen of our states.

The Enemy Within

The communist threat from without may be serious, but it is the enemy within, warns President McKay, that is most menacing. (Jerreld L. Newquist, Prophets, principles, and National Survival (Salt Lake City, Utah, Publishers Press, 1964), p. 229.)

President McKay has said that he would not deal with a nation that treats another as Russia has treated America. (Newquist, op. cit.) Yet, the tragedy is, that one of the major reasons for the rapid growth of communism is because of the help – yes, the increasing help – which they are receiving from right within our own government.

Today our boys are dying in a war with the Communists, a war which our government has not declared – the largest undeclared war in the history of the world – and one which it is alleged our government has no intention of winning. Yet our government encourages us to buy communist goods and our government continues to give aid to the enemy.

One of the tragic results of prolonging the war in Vietnam in that it weakens our economy and gives excuses for more socialistic controls over our people. Of course within the next few days there may be some dramatic moves made in order to placate and deceive the electorate as there was during the so called Cuban missile crisis. But do not be misled.

President McKay has said that the Supreme Court is leading this nation down the road to atheism. (Newquist, op. cit., p. 187) Not only is the court leading this nation down the road to atheism, but in one tragic decision after another they are leading us down the road to communism. One such decision caused Dorthy Healey, Communist spokesman for the West Coast, to rejoice in these words, quote, "This is the greatest victory the Communist party ever had," unquote. The communists have held victory rallies to honor the Supreme Court and its decisions. The Book of Mormon tells us what corrupt judges can do to freedom.

Communists dedicated to the destruction of our government are allowed to teach at our schools, to hold offices in labor unions, to run for public office. Recently an open and avowed leader of the Communist party in one of our states ran for a county office and received over 87,000 votes.

J. Edgar Hoover, the best informed man in government on the Socialist–Communist conspiracy stated:

"We must now face the harsh truth that the objectives of communism are being steadily advanced because many of us do not readily recognize the means used to advance them.... No one who truly understands what it really is can be taken in by it. Yet the individual is handicapped by coming face to face with a conspiracy so monstrous he cannot believe it exists. The American mind simply has not come to a realization of the evil which has been introduced into our midst." (J. Edgar Hoover, The Elks Magazine, August 1956; quoted in Newquist, op. cit., p. 273.)

President McKay has said that this nation has "traveled far into the soul–destroying land of socialism." (Deseret News, "Church News," October 18, 1952, p. 2.) Now if we understand what socialism embraces, then we will realize that this present Congress has passed more socialistic legislation, recommended by a president than probably any other Congress in the history of our Republic.

At this particular moment in history the United States is definitely threatened and every citizen should know about it. The warning of this hour should resound through the corridors of every American institution – schools, churches, the halls of Congress, press, radio and television, and so far as I am concerned, it will resound – with God's help.

Ten Aids to Enemies of Freedom

Our Republic and Constitution are being destroyed while the enemies of freedom are being aided. How? In at least ten ways:

1. By diplomatic recognition and aid, trade and negotiations with the Communists.
2. By disarmament of our military defenses.
3. By destruction of our security laws and the promotion of atheism by decisions of the Supreme Court.
4. By loss of sovereignty and solvency through international commitments and membership in world organizations.
5. By undermining of local law enforcement agencies and Congressional investigating committees.
6. By usurpations by the executive and judicial branches of our Federal Government.
7. By lawlessness in the name of civil rights.
8. By a staggering national debt with inflation and a corruption of the currency.
9. By a multiplicity of executive orders and federal programs which greatly weaken local and state governments.
10. By the sacrifice of American manhood by engaging in wars we apparently have no intention of winning.

We should all be grateful for the patriots of both parties who are trying to withstand this tidal wave of collectivism led by "masters of deceit."

Youth Programs

One regrettable development is the increasing number of government programs embracing our youth. President J. Reuben Clark, Jr., former under-secretary of state, former ambassador, a great constitutional statesman, and counselor to three presidents of the church put it well when he said:

"Our government with its liberty and free institutions will not long survive a government trained and supervised youth.... Such a youth can be a revolutionary machine." (Deseret News, "Church News, " June 15, 1940; quoted in Newquist, op. cit., p. 367.)

And let me warn you, if these programs are fully introduced here in our midst, we will suffer the tragic consequences.

Evidences to Alarm Us

Some of these things strike pretty close to home. Communists or communist-fronters have appeared on our three major university campuses in this state. An identified Communist performed in our Mormon tabernacle. Some of our newspapers have carried columnists with communist-front records or who parrot the communist line, and there are many other evidences both in this state and in our country that should alarm us.

So-called Civil Rights Movement

One of the main thrusts of the Communist drive in America today is through the so-called civil rights movement. Now there is nothing wrong with civil rights – it's what is being done in the name of civil rights that is shocking.

The man who is generally recognized as the leader of the so-called civil rights movement today in America is a man who has lectured at a Communist training school, who has solicited funds through communist sources, who hired a Communist as a top-level aide, who has affiliated with Communist fronts, who is often praised in the Communist press and who unquestionably parallels the Communist line. This same man advocates the breaking of the law and has been described by J. Edgar Hoover as "the most notorious liar in the country." (U.S. News and World Report, November 30, 1964.)

I warn you, unless we wake up soon and do something about the Conspiracy the Communist-inspired civil rights riots of the past will pale into insignificance compared to the bloodshed and destruction that lie ahead in the near future.

Church Members Not to Escape Danger

Do not think the members of the church shall escape. The Lord has assured us that the church will still be here when he comes again. But has the Lord assured us that we can avoid fighting for freedom and still escape unscathed both temporally and spiritually? We could not escape the eternal consequences of our pre-existent position on freedom. What makes us think we can escape it here?

Listen to President Clark's grave warning:

"I say to you with all the soberness I can, that we stand in danger of losing our liberties, and that once lost, only blood will bring them back; and once lost, we of this church will, in order to keep the church going forward, have more sacrifices to make and more persecutions to endure than we have yet known, heavy as our sacrifices and grievous as our persecutions have been." (J. Reuben Clark, Conference Report, April 1944, pp. 115–116; quoted in Newquist, op. cit., p. 89.)

Now that is the price we are going to have to pay unless we can help to reverse the course our country is taking. The Lord does not want us to pay that price, but we will pay it in full if we fail to fight to preserve our freedom. Often the Lord has to send persecutions in order to rebuke and try to purge the unfaithful. He has done it in the past, and He can do it again. If we deserve it – we will get it.

"Next to being one in worshiping God," says President McKay, "there is nothing in this world upon which this church should be more united than in upholding and defending the Constitution of the United States!." (President David O. McKay, 1956, The Instructor 91:34; quoted in Newquist, op. cit., p. 101.)

There are some who would have us believe that the final test of the rightness of a course is whether everyone is united on it. But the church does not seek unity, simply for unities sake. The unity for which the Lord prayed and which President McKay speaks is the only unity which God honors – that is, "unity in righteousness," unity in principle.

We cannot compromise good and evil in an attempt to have peace and unity in the Church, any more than the Lord could have compromised with Satan in order to avoid the War in Heaven.

Think of the impact for good we could have if we all united behind the prophets in preserving our Constitution. Yet witness the sorry spectacle of those presently of our number who have repudiated the inspired counsel of our prophet when he has opposed federal aid to education (Newquist, op. cit., p. 192) and asked support to the right to work laws. (Newquist, op. cit., p. 415, and "Church News," June 26, 1965.)

It is too much to suppose that all the Priesthood at this juncture will unite behind the Prophet in the fight for freedom. Yet we can pray for that day and in the meantime the faithful should strive to be in harmony with the inspired counsel given by His mouthpiece – the prophet – and thus in unity with the Lord – and hence receive peace to their souls.

The more who are united with the Lord and His prophets the greater will be our chances to preserve our families and to live in freedom.

President Clark knew how righteous unity could stop the Communists when he said:

"Now, what has business and industry done about all this revolutionary activity?... Business and industry neither planned nor did anything effective. There was no concerted effort....

"A common cause with a united front would have worked salvation for us. But business officials were afraid of their stock-holders and their outcry against loss of dividends; the lawyers were afraid of getting whipped in the courts, businessmen felt strong vigorous action might further disturb business; bankers shivered at their own shadows.

"So one constitutional right after another yielded without any real contest, our backs getting nearer to the wall with each retreat. It is now purposed that we retreat still further. Is not this suicide? Is there any one so naive as to think that things will right themselves without a fight? There has been no more fight in us than there is in a bunch of sheep, and we have been much like sheep. Freedom was never brought to a people on a silver platter, nor maintained with whisk brooms and lavender sprays.

"And do not think that all these usurpations, intimidations, and impositions are being done to us through inadvertence or mistake; The whole course is deliberately planned and carried out; Its purpose is to destroy the Constitution and our constitutional government; then to bring chaos, out of which the new Statism with its slavery, is to arise, with a cruel, relentless, selfish, ambitious crew in the saddle, riding hard with whip and spur, a red–shrouded band of nightriders for despotism....

"If we do not vigorously fight for our liberties, we shall go clear through to the end of the road and become another Russia or worse...." (J. Reuben Clark, "Church News," September 25, 1959; quoted in Newquist, op. cit., pp. 327s328.)

According to Norman Vincent Peale, "Their was a time when the American people roared like lions for liberty; now they bleat like sheep for security."

"But," some say, "Shouldn't we have confidence in our government officials – don't we owe them allegiance?" To which we respond in the words of President Clark,

"God provided that in this land of liberty, our political allegiance shall run not to individuals, that is, to government officials... the only allegiant we owe as citizens or denizens of the United States, runs to our inspired Constitution which God Himself set up." (J. Reuben Clark, The Improvement Era, 1940, 43:444; quoted in Newquist, op. cit., p. 198.)

Jefferson warned that we should not talk about confidence in men but that we should inhibit their power through the Constitution. In the meantime, we pray for our leaders as we have always been counseled to do.

It is the devils desire that the Lord's priesthood stay asleep while the strings of tyranny gradually and quietly entangle us until, like Gulliver, we awake too late and find that while we could have broken each string separately as it was put upon us, our sleepiness permitted enough strings to bind us to make a rope that enslaves us.

The Role of the Elders

For years we have heard of the role the elders could play in saving the Constitution from total destruction. But how can the elders be expected to save it if they have not studied it and are not sure if it is being destroyed or what is destroying it.

An informed patriotic gentile was dumbfounded when he heard of Joseph Smith's reported prophecy regarding the mission our elders could perform in saving the Constitution. He lived in a Mormon community with nice people who were busily engaged in other activities but had little concern in preserving their freedom. He wondered if maybe a letter should not be sent to President McKay, urging him to release some of the elders from their present Church activities so their would be a few who could help step forward to save the Constitution.

Now it is not so much a case of a man giving up all his other duties to fight for freedom, as it is a case of a man getting his life in balance so he can discharge all of his God-given responsibilities. And of all these responsibilities President McKay has said that we have "no greater immediate responsibility" than "to protect the freedom vouchsafed by the Constitution of the United States."

There is no excuse that can compensate for the loss of liberty.

Satan's Perverse Reasoning

Now Satan is anxious to neutralize the inspired counsel of the Prophet and hence keep the priesthood off-balance, ineffective and inert in the fight for freedom. He does this through diverse means including the use of perverse reasoning.

For example, he will argue, "There is no need to get involved in the fight for freedom – all you need to do is live the gospel." Of course this is a contradiction, because we cannot fully live the gospel and not be involved in the fight for freedom.

We would not say to someone, "There is no need to be baptized – all you need to do is live the gospel." That would be ridiculous because baptism is a part of the gospel.

How would you have reacted if during the War in Heaven someone had said to you, "Look, just do what's right, there is no need to get involved in the fight for free agency." Now it is obvious what the devil is trying to do, but it is sad to see many of us fall for his destructive line.

The cause of freedom is the most basic part of our religion.

Our position on freedom helped get us to this earth, and it can make the difference as to whether we get back home or not.

The "Title of Liberty"

General Moroni, one of the great men of the Book of Mormon, raised the "title of liberty" and on it he inscribed these words:

"In memory of our God, our religion, and freedom, and our peace, our wives, and our children." (Alma 46:12.)

Why didn't he write upon it "just live your religion, there is no need to concern yourselves about your freedom, your peace, your wives or your children."? The reason he didn't was because all these things were a part of his religion as they are of ours.

Listen to what The Book of Mormon had to say about the man who raised the "title of liberty":

"And Moroni was a strong and a mighty man; he was a man of perfect understanding; yea, a man that did not delight in bloodshed; a man whose soul did joy in the liberty and the freedom of his country, and his brethren from bondage and slavery;

"Yea, and he was a man who was firm in the faith of Christ, and he had sworn with an oath to defend his people, his rights, and his country, and his religion even to the loss of his blood." (Alma 48:11,13.)

And then Moroni is paid this high tribute:

"Yea, verily, verily I say unto you, if all men had been and were, and ever would be like unto Moroni, behold the very powers of hell would have been shaken forever; yea the devil would never have power over the hearts of the children of men." (Alma 48:17.)

Now part of the reason why we don't have sufficient Priesthood bearers to save the Constitution, let alone to shake the powers of hell, is, I fear, because unlike Moroni, our souls do not joy in keeping our country free and we are not firm in the faith of Christ, nor have we sworn with an oath to defend our rights.

The Book of Mormon also tells us of some of the perverse reasoning the devil would use in our day to keep the Saints ignorant, complacent and asleep.

"And others will he pacify, and lull them away into carnal security, that they will say: All is well in Zion; yea, Zion prospereth, all is well – and thus the devil cheateth their souls and leadeth them away carefully down to hell." (2 Nephi 28:21.)

Now this reasoning takes several forms. For instance, "Don't worry," say some, "the Lord will take care of us." This is the usual theme of those who believe in faith without works.

Brigham Young said:

"Some may say, "I have faith the Lord will turn them away." What ground have we to hope this? Have I any good reason to say to my Father in heaven, "fight my battles," when he has given me the sword to wield, the arm and the brain that I can fight for myself? Can I ask Him to fight my battles and sit quietly down waiting for Him to do so? I cannot. I can pray the people to harken to wisdom, to listen to counsel; but to ask God to do for me that which I can do for myself is preposterous to my mind." (Journal of Discourses 12:241.)

"Don't you have faith in America?" say others. But America is made up of people – and only righteous patriotic people work to preserve their freedom. The American people's blessings are conditioned on righteousness and nothing else. We have faith in a faithful citizenry.

Need for an Educated Citizenry

"There is no need to learn about communism in order to avoid it," Some argue. But this counsel can help keep our people in ignorance and apparently flies in the face of the inspired counsel of President McKay who said,

"I believe that only through a truly educated citizenry can the ideals that inspired the Founding Fathers of our nation be preserved and perpetuated." ("Church News," March 13, 1954; quoted in Newquist, op. cit., p. 178.)

And then President McKay said that one of the "four fundamental elements in such an education" was the "open and forcible teaching of the facts regarding communism as an enemy to God and to individual freedom." ("Church News," March 13, 1954; quoted in Newquist, op. cit., p. 181.)

Do we teach people to avoid alcohol and tobacco by pointing out its evil effects? Of course we do. Should we then avoid telling people about the evil nature and devious designs of communism – the greatest satanical threat to the spread of God's work?

"Just preach the gospel – that will stop communism," is another neutralizing argument by some. Did teaching the truth stop the War in Heaven or convert Satan and his hosts? Satan himself through his earthly followers is directing the Communist conspiracy and as President Clark said, "You cannot mollify an unconvertible." (J. Reuben Clark, Conference Report, October 1959, p. 46; quoted in Newquist, op. cit., p. 232.)

As members of the Church we have some close quarters to pass through if we are to save our souls. As the Church gets larger some men have increasing responsibility and more and more duties must be delegated. We all have stewardships for which we must account to the Lord.

Unfortunately some men who do not honor their stewardships may have an adverse affect on many people. Often the greater the man's responsibility the more good or evil he can accomplish. The Lord usually gives a man a long enough rope and sufficient time to determine whether that man wants to pull himself into the presence of God or drop off somewhere below.

There are some regrettable things being said and done by some people in the Church today. As President Clark so well warned, "The ravening wolves are amongst us, from our own membership and they, more than any others, are clothed in sheep's clothing because they wear the habiliments of the priesthood.... We should be careful of them."

Sometimes from behind the pulpit, in our classrooms, in our Council meetings and in our church publications we hear, read or witness things that do not square with the truth. This is especially true where freedom is involved. Now do not let this serve as an excuse for your own wrong-doing. The Lord is letting the wheat and the tares mature before he fully purges the Church. He is also testing you to see if you will be misled. The devil is trying to deceive the very elect.

Keep Your Eye on the Prophet

Let me give you a crucial key to help you avoid being deceived. It is this – learn to keep your eye on the Prophet. He is the Lord's mouthpiece and the only man who can speak for the Lord today. Let his inspired counsel take precedence. Let his inspired words be a basis for evaluating the counsel of all lesser authorities. Then live close to the spirit so you may know the truth of all things.

All men are entitled to inspiration, but only one man is the Lords mouthpiece. Some lesser men have in the past, and will in the future, use their offices unrighteously. Some will, ignorantly or otherwise, use it to promote false counsel; some will use it to lead the unwary astray; some will use it to persuade us that all is well in Zion; some will use it to cover and excuse their ignorance. Keep your eye on the Prophet – for the Lord will never permit his Prophet to lead this Church astray.

This is the word of the Lord to us today regarding the President of the Church:

"Wherefore, meaning the church, thou shalt give heed unto all his words and commandments which he shall give unto you as he receiveth them, walking in all holiness before me;

For his words ye shall receive, as if from mine own mouth, in all patience and faith," (D&C 21:4–5.)

A Statement from the Prophet

Now at our last annual conference in April, President McKay issued a statement on communism. It was printed on the editorial page of the June improvement Era and has recently been reprinted by the Deseret Book Company in an attractive folder entitled "Communism: A Statement of the position of the Church of Jesus Christ of Latter-day Saints." Every student and every family in America should have a copy. The cost is five cents each in lots of 100, or three for 25 cents.

Let me quote a few excerpts from that inspired statement and ye who have been misled into believing that you can somehow righteously avoid standing up for freedom – heed his counsel:

"In order that there may be no misunderstanding by bishops, stake presidents, and others regarding members of the Church participating in nonchurch meetings to study and become informed on the Constitution of the United States, Communism, etc., I wish," said President McKay, "to make the following statements that I have been sending out of my office for some time and that have come under question by some stake authorities, bishoprics, and others.

"Church members are at perfect liberty to act according to their own conscience in matters of safeguarding our way of life. They are, of course, encouraged to honor the highest standards of the gospel and to work to preserve their own freedoms. They are free to participate in nonchurch meetings that are held to warn people of the threat of Communism or any other theory or principle that will deprive us of our free agency or individual liberties vouchsafed by the Constitution of the United States.

"The position of this church on the subject of Communism has never changed. We consider it the greatest satanical threat to peace, prosperity, and the spread of God's work among men that exists on the face of the earth."

"In this connection," President McKay continues, "we are constantly being asked to give our opinion concerning various patriotic groups or individuals who are fighting Communism and speaking up for freedom. Our immediate concern, however, is not what parties, groups, or persons, but with principles. We therefore commend and encourage every person and every group who is sincerely seeking to study constitutional principles and awaken a sleeping and apathetic people to the alarming conditions that are rapidly advancing about us. We wish all of our citizens throughout the land were participating in some type of organized self-education in order that they could better appreciate what is happening and know what they can do about it.

"Supporting the FBI, the police, the congressional committees investigating Communism, and various organizations that are attempting to awaken the people through educational means is a policy we warmly endorse for all our people...." (President David O. McKay, The Improvement Era, June 1966, p. 477; Conference Report, April 1966, p. 109)

I bear witness that this Church position given by our inspired leader – our Prophet-leader – is sound, timely and clear. The need for such counsel has never been greater.

Brethren and sisters, I have talked straight to you today. I know I will be abused by some for what I have said, but I want my skirts to be clean.

Some Questions

"Watchman, what of the night?" (Isaiah 21:11) is the cry of the faithful. I have tried to warn you of the darkness that is moving over us and what we can do about it if we will only follow the Prophet.

Have you counted the cost if our countrymen and especially the body of the Priesthood continue to remain complacent, misled through some of our news media, deceived by some of our officials, and perverted by some of our educators?

Are you prepared to see some of your loved ones murdered, your remaining liberties abridged, the Church persecuted, and your eternal reward jeopardized?

An Eyewitness

I have personally witnessed the heart–rending results of the loss of freedom. I have seen it with my own eyes. I have been close to the godless evil of the socialist-communist conspiracy on both sides of the iron curtain, particularly during my years as European Mission President at the close of the war, and today and also during my eight years in the Cabinet.

It may shock you to learn that the first communist cell in government, so far as we know, was organized in the U.S. Department of Agriculture in the 1930's, John Abt was there. It was John Abt whom Oswald, the accused assassin of President Kennedy, requested for his attorney. Harry Dexter White was there. Lee Pressman was there. And communist Alger Hiss, who was the principle architect and first secretary of the United Nations organizing committee, was there also.

I have talked face-to-face with the godless Communist leaders. It may surprise you to learn that I was host to Mr. Khrushchev for a half day, when he visited the United States. Not that I'm proud of it – I opposed his coming then and I still feel it was a mistake to welcome this atheistic murderer as a state visitor. But according to President Eisenhower, Khrushchev had expressed a desire to learn something of American agriculture, and after seeing Russian agriculture I can understand why.

As we talked face-to-face, he indicated that my grandchildren would live under Communism. After assuring him that I expected to do all in my power to assure that his, and all other grandchildren, would live under freedom, he arrogantly declared, in substance:

"You Americans are so gullible. No you won't accept Communism outright, but we'll keep feeding you small doses of socialism until you'll finally wake up and you find you already have Communism. We won't have to fight you. We'll so weaken your economy until you fall like over–ripe fruit into our hands."

And they are ahead of schedule in their devilish scheme.

I stood in Czechoslovakia in 1946 – two citizens of that country came up to me before this meeting – I stood in Czechoslovakia in 1946 and witnessed the ebbing away of freedom resulting in the total loss of liberty to a wonderful people. I visited among the liberty–loving Polish people and talked with their leaders as the insidious freedom–destroying conspiracy moved in, imposing the chains of bondage on a Christian nation.

In both of these freedom–loving nations were members of the Church, striving, as we are, to live the gospel. But did they stop the Communists? Although their numbers were relatively few, the danger to freedom seemed to be far away. Now there are, no doubt, Mormons in Communist slave labor camps.

The Power of the Priesthood

But here in America, the Lord's base of operations – so designated by the Lord himself, though his holy prophets – we of the priesthood – members of his restored Church might well provide the balance of power to save our freedom. Indeed we might, if we go forward as

General Moroni of old, and raise the standard of liberty throughout the land.

My brethren, we CAN do the job that must be done. We can, as a Priesthood, provide the balance of power to preserve our freedom and save this nation from bondage.

The Prophet Joseph Smith is reported to have prophesied the role the Priesthood might play to save our inspired Constitution. Now is the time to move forward courageously – to become alerted, informed and active. We are not just ordinary men. We bear the priesthood and authority of God. We understand the world and God's divine purpose as no other men.

The Gospel and Freedom

The gospel and its preaching can prosper only in an atmosphere of freedom. And now in this critical period, when many pulpits are being turned into pipelines of collectivist propaganda – preaching the social gospel and denying basic principles of salvation – is the time for action.

We know, as do no other people, that the Constitution of the United States is inspired – established by men whom the Lord raised up for that very purpose. We cannot – we must not – shirk our sacred responsibility to rise up in defense of our God–given freedom.

In our day the Lord has declared to his church:

"Verily I say unto you all: arise and shine forth, that thy light may be a standard to the nations; And that the gathering together upon the land of Zion, and upon her stakes, may be for a defense, and for a refuge from the storm, and from wrath when it shall be poured out without mixture upon the whole earth." (D&C 115:5–6.)

Will we of the priesthood "arise and shine"? Will we provide the "defense" and "refuge"? Now is our time and season for corrective and courageous action.

We Have Been Warned

We have been warned again and again and again. The Lords spokesman has consistently raised his voice of warning about the loss of our freedom. Now he that has ears, let him hear, and ye who praise the Lord, learn to also follow His spokesman.

I know not what course others may take, but as for me and my house, we will strive to walk with the Prophet. And the Prophet has said that:

"No greater immediate responsibility rests upon the members of the church, upon all citizens of this republic and of neighboring republics than to protect the freedom vouchsafe by the Constitution of the United States." (*The Instructor*, August 1953.)

In this mighty struggle each of you has a part. Be on the right side. Stand up and be counted. If you get discouraged, remember the words of Edward Everett Hale, when he said:

"I am only one, but I am one.

I can't do everything, but I can do something.

What I can do, that I ought to do,

And what I ought to do,

By the grace of God, I shall do!"

God bless us to heed the oft-repeated counsel of our Prophet-leader, I pray in the name of Jesus Christ. Amen.

CHRIST AND THE CONSTITUTION

Nearly two thousand years ago a perfect man walked the earth: Jesus the Christ. He was the son of a heavenly father and an earthly mother. He is the God of this world, under the Father. He taught men truth, that they might be free. His example and precepts provide the great standard, the only sure way, for all mankind. He became the first and only one who had the power to reunite his body with his spirit after death. By his power all men who have died shall be resurrected. Before him one day we all must stand to be judged by his laws. He lives today and in the not too distant future shall return, in triumph, to subdue his enemies, to reward men according to their deeds, and to assume his rightful role and to rule and reign in righteousness over the entire earth.

Nearly two hundred years ago, some inspired men walked this land of America – not perfect men, but men raised up by the Perfect Man to perform a great work. Foreordained were they, to lay the foundation of this republic, the Lord's base of operations in these latter days. Blessed by the Almighty in their struggle for liberty and independence, the power of heaven rested on these founders as they drafted that great document for governing men, the Constitution of the United States. Like the Ten Commandments, the truths on which the Constitution was based were timeless; and also, as with the Decalogue, the hand of the Lord was in it. They filled their mission well. From them we were endowed with a legacy of liberty – a constitutional republic.

But today the Christian constitutionalist mourns for his country. He sees the spiritual and political faith of his fathers betrayed by wolves in sheep's clothing. He sees the forces of evil increasing in strength and momentum under the leadership of Satan, the archenemy of freedom. He sees the wicked honored and the valiant abused. He senses that his own generation faces Gethsemanes and Valley Forges that may yet rival or surpass the trials of the early apostles and the men of '76. And this gives him cause to reflect on the most basic of fundamentals, the reason for our existence. Once we understand the fundamental purpose for mortality, we may more easily chart a correct course in the perilous seas that are engulfing our nation.

This life is a probation: a probation in which you and I prove our mettle, a probation that has eternal consequences for each of us. And now is our time and season—as every generation has had theirs – to learn our duties and to do them.

The Lord has so arranged things in this life that men are free agents unto themselves to do good or evil. The Lord allows men to go only so far, but the latitude is great enough that some men promote much wickedness and other men much righteousness.

Clearly, there would be little trial of faith if we received our full reward immediately for every goodly deed, or immediate retribution for every sin. But that there will be an eventual reckoning for each, there is no question.

The Lord is displeased with wickedness, and he will help those who oppose it. But he has given all of us freedom to choose, while reserving for himself our final judgment. And herein lies the hope of all Christian constitutionalists. Why? Because the fight for freedom is God's fight, and free agency is an eternal principle. It existed before this world was formed; it will exist forever. Some men may succeed in denying some aspects of this God–given freedom to their fellowmen, but their success is temporary. Freedom is a law of God, an eternal law. And, like any of God's laws, men cannot break it with impunity. They can only break themselves upon it. So as long as a man stands for freedom, he stands with God. Therefore, any man will be eternally vindicated and rewarded who stands for freedom.

Men receive blessings by obedience to God's laws, and without obedience there is no blessing. Before the final triumphal return of the Lord, the question as to whether we may save our constitutional republic is simply based on two factors: the number of patriots and the extent of their obedience.

That the Lord desires to save this nation that he raised up, there is no doubt. But that he leaves it up to us, with his help, is the awful reality.

There is a time and season for all righteous things, and many of life's failures arise when men neither take the time nor find the season to perform their eternal duties. What, then, in this time and season may best equip us to save our Christian constitutional legacy, while at the same time rescuing our own souls? May I humbly submit six suggestions:

1. Spirituality. In the Book of Mormon, sacred to me as scripture, the Lord states that America is a land choice above all others and that it shall remain free so long as the inhabitants worship the God of the land, Jesus Christ.

Certainly spirituality is the foundation upon which any battle against sin and tyranny must be waged. And because this is basically the struggle of the forces of Christ versus antichrist, it is imperative that our people be in tune with the supreme leader of freedom, the Lord our God. Men stay in tune only when their lives are in harmony with God, for apart from God we cannot succeed, but as a partner with God, we cannot fail. We must be in the amoral and immoral world, but not of it.

2. Balance. We have many responsibilities, and one cannot expect the full blessings of a kind Providence if he neglects any major duty.

A man has duties to his church, his home, his country, and his profession or job.

Duty to church: Each man, in communication with God, must determine his responsibility to the Church. This becomes a serious consideration in a day when many pulpits are being turned into pipelines of collectivist propaganda, preaching the social gospel and denying basic principles of salvation. The least any Christian can do is to study daily the word of the Lord and seek divine aid through daily prayer. We invite all men to examine prayerfully The Church of Jesus Christ of Latter-day Saints – the Mormon Church – which I testify is the Church of Christ, restored to the earth and led today by a prophet of God.

Duty to home: Fathers, you cannot delegate your duty as the head of the home. Mothers, train up your children in righteousness; do not attempt to save the world and thus let your own fireside fall apart. For many years now the Mormon Church has advised parents to set aside one night a week when the family meets together for an evening at home. At this time family goals and duties are discussed, spiritual guidance given, and recreation enjoyed. To this end the Church has published and distributes, free of charge, a home evening manual with helpful suggestions for each week's activities.

The duty of parents is to be of help to each other and to their children; then comes their duty to their neighbors, community, nation, and world, in that order. The home is the rock foundation, the cornerstone of civilization. No nation will ever rise above its homes.

Duty to country: No one can delegate his duty to preserve his freedom, for the price of liberty is still eternal vigilance. There are now thousands of businessmen behind the iron curtain who, if they had their lives to live over, would balance their time more judiciously and give more devotion to their civic responsibilities. An ounce of energy in the preservation of freedom is worth a ton of effort to get it back once it is lost.

Duty to job: Every man should provide the necessities of food, clothing, and shelter for his family. As Paul wrote to Timothy: "But if any provide not for his own, and specially for those of his own house, he hath denied the faith, and is worse than an infidel." (1 Tim. 5:8.)

Indolence invites the benevolent straightjacket of the character-destroying welfare state. But a man pays too high a price for worldly success if in his climb to prominence he sacrifices his spiritual, home, and civic responsibilities. How a person should apportion his time among his several duties requires good judgment and is a matter over which each should invite divine assistance.

3. Courageous action. I believe that, while we should ask the Lord's blessings on all our doings and should never do anything upon which we cannot ask his blessings, we should not expect the Lord to do for us what we can do for ourselves. I believe in faith and works, and that the Lord will bless more fully the man who works for what he prays for than he will the man who only prays.

Today you cannot effectively fight for freedom and not be attacked, and those who think they can are deceiving themselves. While I do not believe in stepping out of the path of duty to pick up a cross I do not need, a man is a coward who refuses to pick up a cross that clearly lies within his path.

A man must not only stand for the right principles, but he must also fight for them. Those who fight for principle can be proud of the friends they've gained and the enemies they've earned.

4. Education. We must each of us do our homework. We must be wise as serpents; for, as the apostle Paul said, we wrestle "against the rulers of the darkness..., against spiritual wickedness in high places." (Eph. 6:12.)

We are going through the greatest, most insidious propaganda campaign of all time. Even the character-destroying "credibility gap" seems to be gaining respectability. We cannot believe all we read, and what we can believe is not all of the same value. We must sift. We must learn by study and prayer.

Study the scriptures and study the mortals who have been most consistently accurate about the most important things. When your freedom and your eternal welfare are at stake, your information had better be accurate.

5. Health. To meet and beat the enemy will require clear heads and strong bodies. Hearts and hands grow strong, based on what they are fed. Let us take into our bodies and souls only those things that will make us more effective instruments. We need all the physical, mental, and moral power we can get.

Righteous concern about conditions is commendable when it leads to constructive action. But undue worry is debilitating. When we have done what we can do, then let's leave the rest to God.

Man needs beneficial recreation, a change of pace that refreshes him for heavy tasks ahead. Man also must take time to meditate, to sweep the cobwebs from his mind, so that he might get a more firm grip on the truth and spend less time chasing phantoms and dallying in projects of lesser worth.

Clean hearts and healthful food, exercise, early sleep and fresh air, wholesome recreation and meditation, combined with optimism that comes from fighting for the right and knowing you'll eventually win for keeps–this is the tonic every true Christian patriot needs and deserves.

6. Be Prepared. We have a duty to survive, not only spiritually but also physically. Not survival at the cost of principles, for this is the surest way to defeat, but a survival that comes from intelligent preparation. We face days ahead that will test the moral and physical sinews of all of us.

The scriptural parable of the five wise and the five foolish virgins is a reminder that one can wait too long before he attempts to get his spiritual and temporal house in order. Are we prepared?

A man should not only be prepared to protect himself physically, but he should also have on hand sufficient supplies to sustain himself and his family in an emergency. For many years the leaders of the Mormon Church have recommended, with instructions, that every family have on hand at least a year's supply of basic food, clothing, fuel (where possible), and provisions for shelter. This has been most helpful to families suffering temporary reverses. It can and will be useful in many circumstances in the days ahead. We also need to get out of financial bondage, to be debt free.

Now these suggestions regarding spirituality, balance, courageous action, education, health, and preparation are given not only to help equip one for the freedom struggle, but also to help equip one for eternal life.

Those who hesitate to get into this fight because it is controversial fail to realize that life's decisions should be based on principles, not on public opinion polls.

There were men at Valley Forge who weren't sure how the revolution would end, but they were in a much better position to save their own souls and their country than those timid men whose major concern was deciding which side was going to win, or how to avoid controversy.

The basic purpose of life is to prove ourselves, not to be with the majority when it is wrong. Those who hesitate to get into the fight for freedom because they're not sure if we're going to win fail to realize that we will win in the long run, and for good.

Time is on the side of truth, and truth is eternal. Those who are fighting against freedom and other eternal principles of right may feel confident now, but they are shortsighted.

This is still God's world. The forces of evil, working through some mortals, have made a mess of a good part of it. But it is still God's world. In due time, when each of us has had a chance to prove himself – including whether or not we are going to stand up for freedom – God will interject himself, and the final and eternal victory shall be for free agency. And then shall those weak–willed souls on the sidelines and those who took the wrong but temporarily popular course lament their decisions.

Let us get about our business, for any Christian constitutionalist who retreats from this battle jeopardizes his life here and hereafter. Seldom has so much responsibility hung on so few, so heavily; but our numbers are increasing, and we who have been warned have a responsibility to warn our neighbor.

To his disciples, the Lord said that they should be of good cheer, for he had overcome the world–and so he had. And so can we, if we are allied with him. Time is on the side of truth, and the wave of the future is freedom. There is no question of the eventual, final, and lasting triumph of righteousness. The major question for each of us is what part will we play in helping to bring it to pass.

This is a glorious hour in which to live. Generations past and future will mark well our response to our awesome duty. There is a reason why we have been born in this day. Ours is the task to try to live and perpetuate the principles of the Christ and the Constitution in the face of tremendous odds. May we, with God's help, have strength for the battle and fill our mission in honor for God, family, and country.

The Lord declared that "if ye are prepared ye shall not fear." (D&C 38:39). May we prepare, then fear not, I humbly pray.

BE NOT DECEIVED

Humbly and gratefully I approach you today. Humble in the awesome task of speaking to you – grateful for the gospel and a prophet at our head. I concur in this great address on man and free agency given by the Lord's mouthpiece. President McKay will go down in eternity as one of the great champions of free men.

Years ago my great-grandfather, while an investigator, attended a Mormon meeting during which a member had a quarrel over the Sacrament table with the branch president. When the service was over, Mrs. Benson turned to Ezra T. and asked him what he thought of the Mormons now. I'll always be grateful for his answer. He said he thought the actions of its members in no way altered the truth of Mormonism. That conviction saved him from many a tragedy. Before joining the Church, Grandfather was moved by a marvelous prayer of Apostle John E. Page.

But later the young convert was greatly shocked by the same man whose actions reflected his gradual apostasy.

Ironically, when Elder Page eventually was excommunicated, Brigham Young selected the young convert to fill Elder Page's place in the Quorum of the Twelve.

Six of the original Twelve Apostles selected by Joseph Smith were excommunicated. The Three Witnesses to the Book of Mormon left the Church. Three of Joseph Smith's Counselors fell – one even helped plot his death.

A natural question that might arise would be, that if the Lord knew in advance that these men would fall, as he undoubtedly did, why did he have his Prophet call them to such high office? The answer is; to fill the Lord's purposes. For even the Master followed the will the will of the Father by selecting Judas. President George Q. Cannon suggests an explanation, too, when he states:

"Perhaps it is His own design that faults and weaknesses should appear in high places in order that His Saints may learn to trust in Him and not in any man or men." (Millennial Star 53:658–659. February 15, 1891.)

And this would parallel Lehi's warning; put not your "...trust in the arm of flesh..." (2 Nephi 4:34.)

"The Church," says President McKay, "is little, if at all, injured by persecution and calumnies from ignorant, misinformed, or malicious enemies." (The Instructor, February 1956, p. 33.)

It is from within the Church that the greatest hindrance comes. And so, it seems, it has been. Now the question arises, will we stick with the kingdom and can we avoid being deceived? Certainly this is an important question, for the Lord has said that in the last days the devil will "rage in the hearts of ... men," (2 Nephi 28:20) and if it were possible he shall "deceive the very elect." (See Joseph Smith 1:5–37.)

"The adversary," said Brigham Young, "presents his principles and arguments in the most approved style, and in the most winning tone, attended with the most graceful attitudes; and he is very careful to ingratiate himself into the favour of the powerful and influential of mankind, uniting himself with popular parties, floating into offices of trust and emolument by pandering to popular feeling, though it should seriously wrong and oppress the innocent. Such characters put on the manners of an angel, appearing as nigh like angels of light as they possibly can, to deceive the innocent and the unwary. The good which they do, they do it to bring to pass an evil purpose upon the good and honest followers of Jesus Christ." (JD 11, 238–239.)

Those of us who think "... all is well in Zion ..." (2 Nephi 28:21) in spite of Book of Mormon warning might ponder the words of Heber C. Kimball when he said, "Yes, we think we are secure here in the chambers of these everlasting hills ... but I want to say to you, my brethren, the time is coming when we will be mixed up in these now peaceful valleys to that extent that it will be difficult to tell the face of a Saint from the face of an enemy against the people of God. Then is the time to look out for the great sieve, for there will be a great sifting time, and many will fall. For I say unto you there is a test, a Test, a TEST coming." (Heber C. Kimball, 1856. Quoted by J. Golden Kimball, Conference Report, October 1930, pp. 59–60.)

One of the greatest discourses that I have ever heard or read on how to avoid being deceived was given from this pulpit during the priesthood session of the October, 1960 semiannual conference by Elder Marion G. Romney. (Ibid., October 1960, 73–75.) I commend it to you for your close study and wish that there were time to reread it. During the talk Elder Romney stated that there was no guarantee that the devil will not deceive a lot of men who hold the priesthood. Then, after referring to a talk on free agency by President McKay, Elder Romney states, "... Free agency is the principle against which Satan waged his war in heaven. It is still the front on which he makes his most furious, devious, and persistent attacks. That this would be the case was foreshadowed by the Lord. ..."

And then after quoting the scripture from the Pearl of Great Price regarding the war in heaven over free agency (Moses 4:1–4) Elder Romney continues:

"You see, at the time he was cast out of heaven, his objective was (and still is) 'to deceive and to blind men and to lead them captive at his will.' This he effectively does to as many as will not hearken unto the voice of God. His main attack is still on free agency. When he can get men to yield their agency, he has them well on the way to captivity.

"We who hold the priesthood must beware concerning ourselves, that we do not fall into the traps he lays to rob us of our freedom. We must be careful that we are not led to accept or support in any way any organization, cause or measure which, in its remotest effect, would jeopardize free agency, whether it be in politics, government, religion, employment, education, or any other field. It is not enough for us to be sincere in what we support. We must be right!"

Elder Romney then outlined some tests to distinguish the true from the counterfeit. Now this is crucial for us to know, for as President [John] Taylor said, "Besides the preaching of the Gospel, we have another mission, namely, the perpetuation of the free agency of man and the maintenance of liberty, freedom, and the rights of man." (JD 23, 63.)

It was the struggle over free agency that divided us before we came here; it may well be the struggle over the same principle which will deceive and divide us again.

May I suggest three short tests to avoid being deceived, both pertaining to this freedom struggle and all other matters.

1. What do the standard works have to say about it? "To the law and to the testimony: if they speak not according to this word, it is because there is no light in them," said Isaiah. (Isa. 8:20.) This is one of the great truths of Isaiah so important that it was included in the Book of Mormon scriptures. There it reads: "To the law and to the testimony; and if they speak not according to this word, it is because there is no light in them." (2 Nephi 18:20.) And Hosea said, "My people are destroyed for lack of knowledge: ..." (Hos. 4:6.)

We must diligently study the scriptures. Of special importance to us are the Book of Mormon and the Doctrine and Covenants. Joseph Smith said, "... that the Book of Mormon was the most correct of any book on earth, and the keystone of our religion, and a man would get nearer to God by abiding by its precepts, than by any other book." (DHC 4, 461.)

The Book of Mormon, Brigham Young said, was written on the tablets of his heart and no doubt helped save him from being deceived. The Book of Mormon has a lot to say about America freedom, and secret combinations.

The Doctrine and Covenants is important because it contains the revelations which helped lay the foundation of this great Latter-day work. It speaks of many things. Section 134, verse 2, states that government should hold inviolate the rights and control of property. This makes important reading in a day when government controls are increasing and people are losing the right to control their own property.

2. The second guide is: what do the Latter-day Presidents of the Church have to say on the subject—particularly the living President? President Wilford Woodruff related an instance in church history when Brigham Young was addressing a congregation in the presence of the Prophet Joseph Smith:

"Brother Brigham took the stand, and he took the Bible and laid it down; he took the Book of Mormon, and laid it down: and he took the Book of Doctrine and Covenants, and laid it down before him, and he said, 'There is the written word of God to us, concerning the work of God from the beginning of the world, almost, to our day.' 'And now,' said he 'when compared with the living oracles, those books are nothing to me; those books do not convey the word of God direct to us now, as do the words of a Prophet or a man bearing the Holy Priesthood in our day and generation. I would rather have the living oracles than all the writing in the books.' That was the course he pursued. When he was through, Brother Joseph said to the congregation: 'Brother Brigham has told you the word of the Lord, and he has told you the truth'..." (Conference Report, October 1897, pp. 18–19.)

There is only one man on the earth today who speaks for the Church. (See D&C 132:7, 21:4.) That man is President David O. McKay. Because he gives the word of the Lord for us today, his words have an even more immediate importance than those of the dead prophets. When speaking under the influence of the Holy Ghost his words are scripture. (See D&C 68:4.) I commend for your reading the masterful discourse of President J. Reuben Clark Jr., in the Church News of July 31, 1954, entitled: "When Are Church Leader's Words Entitled to Claim of Scripture?"

The President can speak on any subject he feels is needful for the Saints. As Brigham Young has stated: "I defy any man on earth to point out the path a prophet of God should walk in, or point out his duty, and just how far he must go, in dictating temporal or spiritual things. Temporal and spiritual things are inseparably connected, and ever will be." (JD 10, 364) Other officers in the kingdom have fallen but never the Presidents. Keep your eye on the captain is still good counsel. The words of a living prophet must, and ever will take precedence.

President McKay has said a lot about our tragic trends towards socialism and communism and the responsibilities liberty-loving people have in defending and preserving our Constitution. (See, Conference Report, April 1953, pp. 112–113.) Have we read these words from God's mouthpiece and pondered on them?

3. The third and final test is the Holy Ghost—the test of the Spirit. By that Spirit we "... may know the truth of all things." (Moroni 10:5.) This test can only be fully effective if one's channels of communication with God are clean and virtuous and uncluttered with sin. Said Brigham Young:

"You may know whether you are led right or wrong, as well as you know the way home; for every principle God has revealed carries its own convictions of its truth to the human mind, ...

"What a pity it would be if we were led by one man to utter destruction! Are you afraid of this? I am more afraid that this people have so much confidence in their leaders that they will not inquire of themselves of God whether they are led by Him. I am fearful they settle down in a state of blind self-security, trusting their eternal destiny in the hands of their leaders with a reckless confidence that in itself would thwart the purposes of God in their salvation, and weaken that influence they could give to their leaders did they know for themselves, by the revelations of Jesus, that they are led in the right way. Let every man and woman know, by the whispering of the Spirit of God to themselves, whether their leaders are walking in the path that the Lord dictates, or not. This has been my exhortation continually." (JD 9, 149–150.)

Elder Heber C. Kimball stated: "The time will come when no man or woman will be able to endure on borrowed light." (Orson F. Whitney, Life of Heber C. Kimball, 1888 edition 461.)

How then can we know if a man is speaking by the spirit? The Bible, Book of Mormon, and Doctrine and Covenants give us the key. (See D&C 50:17–23; 100:5–8; 2 Nephi 33:1; 1 Cor. 2:10–11.) President Clark summarized them well when he said:

"We can tell when the speakers are moved upon by the Holy Ghost only when we, ourselves, are moved upon by the Holy Ghost. In a way, this completely shifts the responsibility from them to us to determine when they so speak . . . the Church will know by the testimony of the Holy Ghost in the body of the members, whether the brethren in voicing their views are moved upon by the Holy Ghost; and in due time that knowledge will be made manifest." (Church News, July 31, 1954.)

Will this Spirit be needed to check actions in other situations? Yes, and it could be used as a guide and a protector for the faithful in a situation described by Elder Lee at the last general priesthood session of the Church when he said:

"In the history of the Church there have been times or instances where Counselors in the First Presidency and others in high station have sought to overturn the decision or to persuade the President contrary to his inspired judgment, and always, if you will read carefully the history of the Church, such oppositions brought not only disastrous results to those who resisted the decision of the President, but almost always such temporary persuasions were called back for reconsideration, or a reversal of hasty action not in accordance with the feelings, the inspired feelings, of the President of the Church. And that, I submit, is one of the fundamental things that we must never lose sight of in the building up of the kingdom of God." (Conference Report, April, 1963, p. 81.)

These then, are the three tests: The standard works; the inspired words of the Presidents of the Church, particularly the living Presidents; and the promptings of the Holy Ghost.

Now, brothers and sisters, in this great struggle for free agency just think what a power for good we could be in this world if we were united. Remember how President Clark used to reiterate in the general priesthood meeting of the Church that there was not a righteous thing in this world that we couldn't accomplish if we were just united.

And President McKay has reiterated it again and again when he's stated: "Next to being one in worshiping God, there is nothing in this world upon which this Church should be more united than in upholding and defending the Constitution of the United States!

"May the appeal of our Lord in His intercessory prayer for unity be realized in our homes, our wards, our stakes, and in our support of the basic principles of our Republic," said President McKay. (The Instructor, February 1956. p. 34.)

To that I say Amen and Amen.

President McKay speaks of a unity on principles. President Clark said:

"God provided that in this land of liberty, our political allegiance shall run not to individuals, that is, to government officials, no matter how great or how small they may be. Under His plan our allegiance and the only allegiance we owe as citizens or denizens of the United States, runs to our inspired Constitution which God Himself set up. So runs the oath of office of those who participate in government. A certain loyalty we do owe to the office which a man holds, but even here we owe, just by reason of our citizenship, no loyalty to the man himself. In other countries it is to the individual that allegiance runs. This principle of allegiance to the Constitution is basic to our freedom. It is one of the great principles that distinguishes this 'land of liberty' from other countries.

"Thus God added to His priceless blessings to us.

"I wish to say with all the earnestness I possess that when you youth and maidens see any curtailment of these liberties I have named, when you see government invading any of these realms of freedom which we have under our Constitution, you will know that they are putting shackles on your liberty, and that tyranny is creeping upon you, no matter who curtails these liberties or who invades these realms, and no matter what the reason and excuse therefore may be." (The Improvement Era, 43, [July 1940] 444.)

We all should know by now what President McKay has said about liberty–loving peoples' greatest responsibility. We've heard him tell of our drift toward socialism and communism. We know of his feelings regarding recent tragic decisions of the Supreme Court. We know the Church's position supporting right to work laws and the Church's opposition to programs of federal aid to education. These and many more things has President McKay told us that involve the great struggle against state slavery and the anti-Christ. Now, inasmuch as all these warnings have come through the only mouthpiece of the Lord on the earth today there is one major question we should ask ourselves. Assuming we are living a life so we can know, then what does the Holy Spirit have to say about it?

We are under obligation to answer this question. God will hold us responsible.

Let us not be deceived in the sifting days ahead. Let us rally together on principle behind the prophet as guided by the promptings of the Spirit.

We should continue to speak out for freedom and against socialism and communism as President McKay has consistently admonished us. We should continue to come to the aid of patriots, programs and organizations which are trying to save our Constitution through every legal and moral means possible.

God has not left us in darkness regarding these matters. We have the scriptures ancient and modern. We have a living prophet, and we may obtain the Spirit.

Joseph Smith did see the Father and the Son. The kingdom established through the Prophet's instrumentality will roll forth.

We can move forward with it.

That we may all do so and be not deceived is my humble prayer. In the name of Jesus Christ. Amen.

WATCHMAN, WARN THE WICKED

The prophet Ezekiel declared: "Son of man, I have made thee a watchman unto the house of Israel: therefore hear the word at my mouth, and give them warning from me.

"When I say unto the wicked, Thou shalt surely die; and thou givest him not warning, nor speakest to warn the wicked from his wicked way, to save his life; the same wicked man shall die in his iniquity; but his blood will I require at thine hand.

"Yet if thou warn the wicked, and he turn not from his wickedness, nor from his wicked way, he shall die in his iniquity; but thou hast delivered thy soul." (Ezek. 3:17–19.)

The inspired Book of Mormon prophets saw our day and warned us of the strategy of the adversary. Hear their words:

"For behold, at that day shall he [the devil] rage in the hearts of the children of men, and stir them up to anger against that which is good.

"And others will he pacify, and lull them away into carnal security...

"... wo be unto him that hearkeneth unto the precepts of men, and denieth the power of God. (2 Ne. 28:20–21, 26.)

Through a modern prophet, Joseph Smith, the Lord has given this further warning: "Wherefore the voice of the Lord is unto the ends of the earth, that all that will hear may hear:

". . . and the day cometh that they who will not hear the voice of the Lord, neither the voice of his servants, neither give heed to the words of the prophets and apostles, shall be cut off from among the people;

"For they have strayed from mine ordinances, and have broken mine everlasting covenant;

"They seek not the Lord to establish his righteousness, but every man walketh in his own way, and after the image of his own God, whose image is in the likeness of the world...

"What I the Lord have spoken, I have spoken, and I excuse not myself; and though the heavens and the earth pass away, my word shall not pass away, but shall all be fulfilled, whether by mine own voice, or by the voice of my servants, it is the same." (D&C 1:11, 14–16, 38.)

These warnings were given 140 years ago. The fulfillment is now. We are living witnesses, unless we are blinded by our own complacency and the craftiness of evil men.

As watchmen on the tower of Zion, it is our obligation and right as leaders to speak out against current evils – evils that strike at the very foundation of all we hold dear as the true church of Christ and as members of Christian nations.

As one of these watchmen, with a love for humanity, I accept humbly this obligation and challenge and gratefully strive to do my duty without fear. In times as serious as these, we must not permit fear of criticism to keep us from doing our duty, even at the risk of our counsel being tabbed as political, as government becomes more and more entwined in our daily lives.

In the crisis through which we are now passing, we have been fully warned. This has brought forth some criticism. There are some of us who do not want to hear the message. It embarrasses us. The things which are threatening our lives, our welfare, our freedoms are the very things some of us have been condoning. Many do not want to be disturbed as they continue to enjoy their comfortable complacency.

The Church is founded on eternal truth. We do not compromise principle. We do not surrender our standards regardless of current trends or pressures. Our allegiance to truth as a church is unwavering.

Speaking out against immoral or unjust actions has been the burden of prophets and disciples of God from time immemorial. It was for this very reason that many of them were persecuted. Nevertheless, it was their God-given task, as watchmen on the tower, to warn the people.

We live in an age of appeasement – the sacrificing of principle. Appeasement is not the answer. It is never the right answer.

One of these modern Church watchmen has given this sound warning:

"A milk-and-water allegiance kills; while a passionate devotion gives life and soul to any cause and its adherents. The troubles of the world may largely be laid at the doors of those who are neither hot nor cold; who always follow the line of least resistance; whose timid hearts flutter at taking sides for truth. As in the great Council in the heavens, so in the Church of Christ on earth, there can be no neutrality. We are, or we are not, on the side of the Lord. An unrelenting faith, contemptuous of all compromise, will lead the Church and every member of it, to triumph and the achievement of our high destiny.

"The final conquerors of the world will be the men and women, few or many matters not, who fearlessly and unflinchingly cling to truth, and who are able to say no, as well as yes, on whose lofty banner is inscribed: No compromise with error...

"Tolerance is not conformity to the world's view and practices. We must not surrender our beliefs to get along with people, however beloved or influential they may be. Too high a price may be paid for social standing or even for harmony... The Gospel rests upon eternal truth; and truth can never be deserted safely." (John A. Widtsoe, Conference Report, April 1941, pp. 117, 116.)

It has been well said that "our greatest national problem is erosion. Not erosion of the soil, but erosion of the national morality."

The United States of America has been great because it has been free. It has been free because it has trusted in God and was founded upon the principles of freedom set forth in the word of God. This nation has a spiritual foundation. To me, this land has a prophetic history.

In the year 1831 Alexis de Tocqueville, the famous French historian, came to our country at the request of the French government to study our penal institutions. He also made a close study of our political and social institutions. In less than ten years, de Tocqueville had become world–famous, as the result of the four-volume work that he wrote, entitled Democracy in America. Here is his own stirring explanation of the greatness of America:

"I sought for the greatness and genius of America in her commodious harbors and her ample rivers, and it was not there; in her fertile fields and boundless prairies, and it was not there; in her rich mines and her vast world commerce, and it was not there. Not until I went to the churches of America and heard her pulpits aflame with righteousness did I understand the secret of her genius and power. America is great because she is good, and if America ever ceases to be good, America, will cease to be great." (Prophets, Principles and National Survival, compiled by Jerreld L. Newquist [Salt Lake City, Publishers Press, 1964], p. 60.)

How strong is our will to remain free – to be good? False thinking and false ideologies, dressed in the most pleasing forms, quietly – almost without our knowing it – seek to reduce our moral defenses and to captivate our minds. They entice with bright promises of security, cradle-to-grave guarantees of many kinds. They masquerade under various names, but all may be recognized by one thing one thing they all have in common: to erode away character and man's freedom to think and act for himself.

Effort will be made to lull us away into a false security. Proposals will be and are being offered and programs sponsored that have wide appeal. Attractive labels are usually attached to the most dangerous programs, often in the name of public welfare and personal security. Again, let us not be misled.

Freedom can be killed by neglect as well as by direct attack.

Too long have too many Americans, and people of the free world generally, stood by as silent accessories to the crimes of assault against freedom assault against basic economic and spiritual principles and traditions that have made nations strong.

Let us strive for progress down the road of goodness and freedom. With the help and blessings of the Lord, the free people of the United States and the free world can and will face tomorrow without fear, without doubt, and with full confidence. We do not fear the phony population explosion, nor do we fear a shortage of food, if we can be free and good. The Lord has declared, "... the earth is full, and there is enough and to spare. ..." (D&C 104:17.) We can accept this promise with confidence.

President Calvin Coolidge pinpointed the problem some years ago with these words:

"We do not need more material development, we need more spiritual development. We do not need more intellectual power, we need more moral power. We do not need more knowledge, we need more character. We do not need more government, we need more culture. We do not need more law, we need more religion. We do not need more of the things that are seen, we need more of the things that are unseen. It is on that side of life that it is desirable to put the emphasis at the present time. If that side is strengthened, the other side will take care of itself. It is that side which is the foundation of all else. If the foundation be firm, the superstructure will stand." (Prophets, Principles and National Survival p. 35.)

As a free people, we are following very closely in many respects the pattern which led to the downfall of the great Roman Empire. A group of well-known historians has summarized those conditions leading to the downfall of Rome in these words:

"... Rome had known a pioneer beginning not unlike our own pioneer heritage, and then entered into two centuries of greatness, reaching its pinnacle in the second of those centuries, going into the decline and collapse in the third. Yet, the sins of decay were becoming apparent in the latter years of that second century.

"It is written that there were vast increases in the number of the idle rich, and the idle poor. The latter (the idle poor) were put on a permanent dole, a welfare system not unlike our own. As this system became permanent, the recipients of public largesse (welfare) increased in number. They organized into a political block with sizable power.

They were not hesitant about making their demands known. Nor was the government hesitant about agreeing to their demands and with ever-increasing frequency. Would-be emperors catered to them. The great, solid middle class – Rome's strength then as ours is today was taxed more and more to support a bureaucracy that kept growing larger, and even more powerful. Surtaxes were imposed upon incomes to meet emergencies. The government engaged in deficit spending. The denarius, a silver coin similar to our half dollar, began to lose its silvery hue. It took on a copper color as the government reduced the silver content.

"Even then, Gresham's law was at work, because the real silver coin soon disappeared. It went into hiding.

"Military service was an obligation highly honored by the Romans. Indeed, a foreigner could win Roman citizenship simply by volunteering for service in the legions of Rome. But, with increasing affluence and opulence, the young men of Rome began avoiding this service, finding excuses to remain in the soft and sordid life of the city. They took to using cosmetics and wearing feminine–like hairdos and garments, until it became difficult, the historians tell us, to tell the sexes apart.

"Among the teachers and scholars was a group called the Cynics whose number let their hair and beards grow, and who wore slovenly clothes, and professed indifference to worldly goods as they heaped scorn on what they called `middle class values.'

"The morals declined. It became unsafe to walk in the countryside or the city streets. Rioting was commonplace and sometimes whole sections of towns and cities were burned.

"And, all the time, the twin diseases of confiscatory taxation and creeping inflation were waiting to deliver the death blow.

"Then finally, all these forces overcame the energy and ambition of the middle class.

"Rome fell.

"We are now approaching the end of our second century." (Address by Governor Ronald Reagan of California at Eisenhower College, New York, 1969.)

In 1787 Edward Gibbon completed his noble work *The Decline and Fall of the Roman Empire*. Here is the way he accounted for the fall:

1. The undermining of the dignity and sanctity of the home, which is the basis of human society.
2. Higher and higher taxes and the spending of public monies for free bread and circuses for the populace.
3. The mad craze for pleasure, sports becoming every year more and more exciting and brutal.
4. The building of gigantic armaments when the real enemy was within the decadence of the people.
5. The decay of religion – faith fading into mere form, losing touch with life, and becoming impotent to warn and guide the people.

Is there a parallel for us in America today? Could the same reasons that destroyed Rome destroy America and possibly other countries of the free world?

For eight years in Washington I had this prayerful statement on my desk: "O God, give us men with a mandate higher than the ballot box."

The lessons of history, many of them very sobering, ought to be turned to during this hour of our great achievements, because during the hour of our success is our greatest danger. Even during the hour of our great prosperity, a nation may sow the seeds of its own destruction. History reveals that rarely is a great civilization conquered from without unless it has weakened or destroyed itself within.

The lessons of history stand as guideposts to help us safely chart the course for the future.

As American citizens, as citizens of the nations of the free world, we need to rouse ourselves to the problems which confront us as great Christian nations. We must recognize that these fundamental, basic principles moral and spiritual lay at the very foundation of our past achievements. To continue to enjoy present blessings, we must return to these basic and fundamental principles. Economics and morals are both part of one inseparable body of truth. They must be in harmony. We need to square our actions with these eternal verities.

The Church of Jesus Christ of Latter-day Saints stands firm in support of the great spiritual and moral principles which have been the basic traditions of the free world. We oppose every evil effort to downgrade or challenge the eternal verities which have undergirded civilization from the beginning.

We will use every honorable means to strengthen the home and family; to encourage obedience to the first and great commandment to multiply and replenish the earth through noble parenthood; and to strengthen character through adherence to high spiritual and moral principles.

In The Church of Jesus Christ of Latter-day Saints chastity will never be out of date. We have one standard for men and women, and that standard is moral purity. We oppose and abhor the damnable practice of wholesale abortion and every other unholy and impure act which strikes at the very foundation of the home and family, our most basic institutions.

A continuation of these immoral practices will surely bring down the wrath and judgments of the Almighty.

In our concentration upon materialism and material acquisitions, are we forgetting the spiritual basis upon which our prosperity, security, and freedom rest? God help us to repent of our evil ways and humble ourselves before the offended power.

There is great safety in a nation on its knees.

What assurance it would give of the much-needed blessings of the Lord if the American people, and people everywhere, could all be found daily night and morning on their knees expressing gratitude for blessings already received, acknowledging our dependence upon God, and seeking his divine guidance.

The spectacle of a nation praying is more awe–inspiring, more powerful, than the explosion of an atomic bomb. The force of prayer is greater than any possible combination of man-controlled powers, because "prayer is man's greatest means of tapping the resources of God." The Founding Fathers accept this eternal verity. Do we? Will we?

Yes, it is in our own enlightened self-interest to engage in this simple practice, this powerful practice of prayer. Roger Babson said many years ago: "What this country needs more than anything else is old-fashioned family prayer." Yes, our greatest need is a return to the old-fashioned, time-tested verities.

God help us, as free men, to recognize the source of our blessings, the threat to our freedom and our moral and spiritual standards, and the need for humble, yet courageous action to preserve these priceless. time-tested blessings. I humbly pray in the name of Jesus Christ. Amen.

NOT COMMANDED IN ALL THINGS

In 1831 the Lord said this to his Church:

"For behold, it is not meet that I should command in all things; for he that is compelled in all things, the same is a slothful and not a wise servant; wherefore he receiveth no reward.

"Verily I say, men should be anxiously engaged in a good cause and do many things of their own free will, and bring to pass much righteousness;

"For the power is in them, wherein they are agents unto themselves. And inasmuch as men do good they shall in nowise lose their reward.

"But he that doeth not anything until he is commanded, and receiveth a commandment with doubtful heart and keepeth it with slothfulness, the same is damned." (D&C 58:26–29.)

The purposes of the Lord–the great objectives–continue the same: the salvation and exaltation of his children.

Objectives and Guide Lines

Usually the Lord gives us the overall objectives to be accomplished and some guidelines to follow, but he expects us to work out most of the details and methods. The methods and procedures are usually developed through study and prayer and by living so that we can obtain and follow the promptings of the Spirit. Less spiritually advanced people, such as those in the days of Moses, had to be commanded in many things. Today those spiritually alert look at the objectives, check the guidelines laid down by the Lord and his prophets, and then prayerfully act – without having to be commanded "in all things." This attitude prepares men for godhood.

The overall objective to be accomplished in missionary work, temple work, providing for the needy, and bringing up our children in righteousness has always been the same; only our methods to accomplish these objectives have varied. Any faithful member in this dispensation, no matter when he lived, could have found righteous methods to have carried out these objectives without having to wait for the latest, specific church-wide program.

Children To Act on Their Own Initiative and Responsibility

Sometimes the Lord hopefully waits on his children to act on their own, and when they do not, they lose the greater prize, and the Lord will either drop the entire matter and let them suffer the consequences or else he will have to spell it out in greater detail. Usually, I fear, the more he has to spell it out, the smaller is our reward.

Often, because of circumstances, the Lord, through revelation to his prophets or through inspired programs designed by faithful members which later become adopted on a church-wide basis, will give to all the membership a righteous means to help accomplish the objective; for instance, any member of the Church a century ago who studied church doctrine would have known that he had the prime responsibility to see that his children had spiritualized family recreation and were taught in the home lessons in character building and gospel principles. But some did not do it.

The Home Evening

Then, in 1915 President Joseph F. Smith introduced, church-wide, the "weekly home evening program" with promised blessings to all who faithfully adopted it. Many refused and lost the promised blessings. (At the October conference, 1947, I referred to that promise in a talk on the Family Home Evening.) Today we have the home evening manual and other helps. Yet some still refuse to bring up their children in righteousness.

But there are some today who complain that the home evening manual should have been issued years ago. If this is true then the Lord will hold his servants accountable, but no one can say that from the inception of the Church up to the present day the Lord through his Spirit to the individual members and through his spokesmen the prophets, has not given us the objectives and plenty of guidelines and counsel. The fact that some of us have not done much about it even when it is spelled out in detail is not the Lord's fault.

For years we have been counseled to have on hand a year's supply of food. Yet there are some today who will not start storing until the Church comes out with a detailed monthly home storage program. Now suppose that never happens. We still cannot say we have not been told.

Should the Lord decide at this time to cleanse the Church – and the need for that cleansing seems to be increasing – a famine in this land of one year's duration could wipe out a large percentage of slothful members, including some ward and stake officers. Yet we cannot say we have not been warned.

Another warning: You and I sustain one man on this earth as God's mouthpiece – President David O. McKay – one of the greatest seers who has ever walked this earth. We do not need a prophet – we have one – what we desperately need is a listening ear.

Warnings of Threats to Freedom

Should it be of concern to us when the mouthpiece of the Lord keeps constantly and consistently raising his voice of warning about the loss of our freedom as he has over the years? There are two unrighteous ways to deal with his prophetic words of warning: you can fight them or you can ignore them. Either course will bring you disaster in the long run.

Hear his words: "No greater immediate responsibility rests upon members of the Church, upon all citizens of this Republic and of neighboring Republics than to protect the freedom vouchsafed by the Constitution of the United States." (Cited in Jerreld L. Newquist, Prophets, Principles and National Survival [SLC: Publishers Press, 1964], p. 157.) As important as are all other principles of the gospel, it was the freedom issue which determined whether you received a body. To have been on the wrong side of the freedom issue during the war in heaven meant eternal damnation. How then can Latter-day Saints expect to be on the wrong side in this life and escape the eternal consequences? The war in heaven is raging on earth today. The issues are the same: "Shall men be compelled to do what others claim is for their best welfare" or will they heed the counsel of the prophet and preserve their freedom?

Satan argued that men given their freedom would not choose correctly therefore he would compel them to do right and save us all. Today Satan argues that men given their freedom do not choose wisely; therefore a so-called brilliant, benevolent few must establish the welfare government and force us into a greater socialistic society. We are assured of being led into the promised land as long as we let them put a golden ring in our nose. In the end we lose our freedom and the promised land also. No matter what you call it – communism, socialism, or the welfare state – our freedom is sacrificed. We believe the gospel is the greatest thing in the world; why then do we not force people to join the Church if they are not smart enough to see it on their own? Because this is Satan's way not the Lord's plan. The Lord uses persuasion and love.

Hear again the words of God's mouthpiece:

"Today two mighty forces are battling for the supremacy of the world. The destiny of mankind is in the balance. It is a question of God and liberty, or atheism and slavery...

"Those forces are known and have been designated by Satan on the one hand, and Christ on the other.

"In Joshua's time they were called 'gods of the Amorites,' for one, and 'the Lord' on the other... In these days, they are called 'domination by the state,' on one hand, 'personal liberty,' on the other; communism on one, free agency on the other." (Ibid., pp. 215–216.)

Now, the Lord knew that before the gospel could flourish there must first be an atmosphere of freedom. This is why he first established the Constitution of this land through gentiles whom he raised up before he restored the gospel. In how many communist countries today are we doing missionary work, building chapels, etc.? And yet practically every one of those countries have been pushed into communism and kept under communism with the great assistance of evil forces which have and are operating within our own country and neighboring lands.

Yes, were it not for the tragic policies of governments – including our own – tens of millions of people murdered and hundreds of millions enslaved since World War II would be alive and free today to receive the restored gospel.

President J. Reuben Clark, Jr., put it clearly and courageously when he said:

"Reduced to its lowest terms, the great struggle which now rocks the whole earth more and more takes on the character of a struggle of the individual versus the state...

"This gigantic world-wide struggle, more and more takes on the form of a war to the death. We shall do well and wisely so to face and so to enter it. And we must all take part. Indeed, we all are taking part in that struggle. whether we will or not. Upon its final issue, liberty lives or dies... The plain and simple issue now facing us in America is freedom or slavery... We have largely lost the conflict so far waged. But there is time to win the final victory, if we sense our danger and fight." (Ibid., pp. 318, 327–328.)

Now where do we stand in this struggle, and what are we doing about it?

The devil knows that if the elders of Israel should ever wake up, they could step forth and help preserve freedom and extend the gospel. Therefore the devil has concentrated, and to a large extent successfully, in neutralizing much of the priesthood. He has reduced them to sleeping giants. His arguments are clever.

Here are a few samples:

First: "We really haven't received much instruction about freedom," the devil says. This is a lie, for we have been warned time and again. No prophet of the Lord has ever issued more solemn warning than President David O. McKay. Last conference I spoke of a book embodying much of the prophets' warnings on freedom from Joseph Smith to David O. McKay which I commend to you. It is entitled *Prophets, Principles, and National Survival.*

Second: "You're too involved in other church work," says the devil. But freedom is a weighty matter of the law; the lesser principles of the gospel you should keep but not leave this one undone. We may have to balance and manage our time better. Your other church work will be limited once you lose your freedom as our Saints have found out in Czechoslovakia, Poland, and many other nations.

Third: "You want to be loved by everyone," says the devil, "and this freedom battle is so controversial you might be accused of engaging in politics." Of course the government has penetrated so much of our lives that one can hardly speak for freedom without being accused of being political. Some might even call the war in heaven a political struggle – certainly it was controversial. Yet the valiant entered it with Michael. Those who support only the popular principles of the gospel have their reward. And those who want to lead the quiet, retiring life but still expect to do their full duty can't have it both ways.

Said Elder John A. Widtsoe:

"The troubles of the world may largely be laid at the doors of those who are neither hot nor cold; who always follow the line of least resistance; whose timid hearts flutter at taking sides for truth. As in the great Council in the heavens, so in the Church of Christ on earth, there can be no neutrality." (Ibid, p. 440.)

Fourth: "Wait until it becomes popular to do," says the devil, "or, at least until everybody in the Church agrees on what should be done." But this fight for freedom might never become popular in our day. And if you wait until everybody agrees in this Church, you will be waiting through the second coming of the Lord. Would you have hesitated to follow the inspired counsel of the Prophet Joseph Smith simply because some weak men disagreed with him? God's living mouthpiece has spoken to us–are we for him or against him? In spite of the Prophet's opposition to increased federal aid and compulsory unionism, some church members still champion these freedom destroying programs. Where do you stand?

Fifth: "It might hurt your business or your family," says the devil, "and besides why not let the gentiles save the country? They aren't as busy as you are." Well, there were many businessmen who went along with Hitler because it supposedly helped their business. They lost everything. Many of us are here today because our forefathers loved truth enough that they fought at Valley Forge or crossed the plains in spite of the price it cost them or their families. We had better take our small pain now than our greater loss later. There were souls who wished afterwards that they had stood and fought with Washington and the founding fathers, but they waited too long – they passed up eternal glory. There has never been a greater time than now to stand up against entrenched evil. And while the gentiles established the Constitution, we have a divine mandate to preserve it. But unfortunately today in this freedom struggle, many gentiles are showing greater wisdom in their generation than the children of light.

Sixth: "Don't worry," says the devil "the Lord will protect you, and besides the world is so corrupt and heading toward destruction at such a pace that you can't stop it, so why try." Well to begin with, the Lord will not protect us unless we do our part. This devilish tactic of persuading people not to get concerned because the Lord will protect them no matter what they do is exposed by the Book of Mormon. Referring to the devil, it says, "And others will he pacify, and lull them away into carnal security, and they will say: All is well in Zion, yea, Zion prospereth, all is well – and thus the devil cheateth their souls, and leadeth them away carefully down to hell." (2 Nephi 28:21.)

I like that word "carefully." In other words, don't shake them, you might awake them. But the Book of Mormon warns us that when we should see these murderous conspiracies in our midst that we should awake to our awful situation. Now why should we awake if the Lord is going to take care of us anyway? Now let us suppose that it is too late to save freedom. It is still accounted unto us for righteousness' sake to stand up and fight. Some Book of Mormon prophets knew of the final desolate end of their nations, but they still fought on, and they saved some souls including their own by so doing. For, after all, the purpose of life is to prove ourselves, and the final victory will be for freedom.

But many of the prophecies referring to America's preservation are conditional. That is, if we do our duty we can be preserved, and if not then we shall be destroyed. This means that a good deal of the responsibility lies with the priesthood of this Church as to what happens to America and as to how much tragedy can be avoided if we do act now.

And now as to the last neutralizer that the devil uses most effectively – it is simply this: "Don't do anything in the fight for freedom until the Church sets up its own specific program to save the Constitution." This brings us right back to the scripture I opened with today – to those slothful servants who will not do anything until they are "compelled in all things." Maybe the Lord will never set up a specific church program for the purpose of saving the Constitution. Perhaps if he set one up at this time it might split the Church asunder, and perhaps he does not want that to happen yet for not all the wheat and tares are fully ripe.

The Prophet Joseph Smith declared it will be the elders of Israel who will step forward to help save the Constitution, not the Church. And have we elders been warned? Yes, we have. And have we elders been given the guide lines? Yes indeed, we have. And besides, if the Church should ever inaugurate a program, who do you think would be in the forefront to get it moving? It would not be those who were sitting on the sidelines prior to that time or those who were appeasing the enemy. It would be those choice spirits who, not waiting to be "commanded in all things," used their own free will, the counsel of the prophets and the Spirit of the Lord as guidelines and who entered the battle "in a good cause" and brought to pass much righteousness in freedom's cause.

Years ago Elder Joseph F. Merrill of the Council of the Twelve encouraged the members of the Church to join right-to-work leagues and President Heber J. Grant concurred. For our day President David

O. McKay has called communism the greatest threat to the Church, and it is certainly the greatest mortal threat this country has ever faced. What are you doing to fight it?

"The War in Heaven" Is Raging on Earth Today

Brethren, if we had done our homework and were faithful, we could step forward at this time and help save this country. The fact that most of us are unprepared to do it is an indictment we will have to bear. The longer we wait, the heavier the chains, the deeper the blood, the more the persecution and the less we can carry out our God-given mandate and world-wide mission. The war in heaven is raging on earth today. Are you being neutralized in the battle?

"Verily I say, men should be anxiously engaged in a good cause and do many things of their own free will, and bring to pass much righteousness; For the power is in them, wherein they are agents unto themselves. ..." (D&C 58:27–28.)

In the name of Jesus Christ. Amen.

RIGHTEOUSNESS EXALTETH A NATION

"Righteousness exalteth a nation."

This statement of eternal truth from Proverbs appeared on the flyleaf and the last page of a booklet at each plate at the President's Prayer Breakfast in the Grand Ballroom of the Mayflower Hotel in Washington, D.C., on February 7, 1963.

As I listened to the prayers, readings from the Old and New Testaments, and messages from government and nongovernment leaders, I reviewed hurriedly our spiritual background as a nation and today's spiritual needs. For truly, "Righteousness exalteth a nation: but sin is a reproach to any people." (Prov. 14:34.)

The beautiful old print that hangs in Carpenter's Hall, Philadelphia, came to mind. It is captioned "The First Prayer in Congress, September 1774." It depicts most of the members of that Congress on their knees with George Washington, our first President, as leader.

I recalled the terrible winter at Valley Forge and Washington on his knees in the snow, praying for divine aid. I thought of the words of Abraham Lincoln during another time of crisis as he said humbly: "I have been driven many times to my knees by the overwhelming conviction that I had nowhere else to go."

Washington acknowledged God's direction and stated, "Of all the dispositions and habits which lead to political prosperity, religion and morality are indispensable supports... Reason and experience both forbid us to expect that national morality can prevail in exclusion of religious principles." (Farewell address.)

Lincoln knew that God rules in the affairs of men and nations. He solemnly declared: "God rules this world. It is the duty of nations as well as men to own their dependence upon the overruling power of God, to confess their sins and transgressions in humble sorrow ... and to recognize the sublime truth that those nations only are blessed whose God is the Lord."

The founding fathers knew that "where the Spirit of the Lord is, there is liberty." (2 Cor. 3:17.) The United States of America began and lives as a result of faith in God. The Bible has been and is the foundation for this faith.

"It is impossible to govern the world without the Bible," said George Washington.

"The Bible is the rock on which this Republic rests," Andrew Jackson proclaimed.

The fathers of our country had to turn to religion in order that their new experiment would make sense.

As I left the prayer breakfast, bidding goodbye to many warm friends, I thought of the greatness of America, the world's greatest power. During World War II she out-produced both her enemies and her allies – "the American miracle."

But I also recalled FBI reports that revealed an ever-increasing crime record. I recalled our shockingly defiant record of drunkenness and immorality and the fact that we have become a nation of pleasure-seeking Sabbath breakers.

My thoughts turned to our homes and families, our ever-increasing divorce rate, the alarming increase in sexual sin, infidelity, yes, even adultery. We live in a day of slick, quiet, and clever sins. It is made easy to cover up.

I recalled the solidarity of the homes of long past when family prayer, daily devotion, the reading of scriptures, and the singing of hymns were common practices in American homes – practices that, I am sorry to say, have all but disappeared today.

I became saddened as I reviewed evidence of a lessening of moral stability, honor, integrity, love of country; a seeking for the honors of men, of something for nothing; the tendency to lean more and more on government; the result of our ever-increasing demands, even though often economically, socially, and spiritually unsound.

There has been a nationwide erosion of individual character. Jefferson's words still ring true: "Material abundance without character is the surest way to destruction." I recalled how proudly in generations past we spoke of the "American way of life."

Then I saw thirty million doorknob hangers being distributed by Scouts, setting forth our political and economic rights in an effort to stimulate patriotism in this choice land. As I read the message from the Freedom Foundation and the Scouts, I thought of our basic American concepts, our constitutional government, based on a fundamental belief in God.

I became alarmed as I reviewed what has happened in our schools under so-called progressive education. What about the loss of patriotism, faith in God, and the teachings of character-building principles once so much a part of our education? We have all but "forced Americanism out of the classroom to make way for temporary trivialities." (De Love.)

I remember President Joseph F. Smith's warning of the three dangers to the Church from within, viz., the flattery of prominent men, sexual impurity, and false educational ideas. (Gospel Doctrine, p. 312.)

Then there came to me the words of that courageous American patriot, J. Edgar Hoover:

"Today as never before, America has need for men and women who possess the moral strength and courage of our forefathers – modern-day patriots, with pride in our country and faith in freedom...

"Too often in recent years, patriotic symbols have been shunted aside. Our national heroes have been maligned, our history distorted. Has it become a disgrace to pledge allegiance to our flag – or sign a loyalty oath, or pay tribute to our national anthem? Is it shameful to encourage our children to memorize the stirring words of the men of '76? Is it becoming opprobrious to state "In God we trust" when proclaiming our love of country?

"What we desperately need today is patriotism founded on a real understanding of the American ideal – a dedicated belief in our principles of freedom, and a determination to perpetuate America's heritage." (FBI Law Enforcement Bulletin, April 1962, p. 3.)

Are we slipping from our moorings, becoming soft, carelessly drawing away from the course that has brought us such priceless blessings in days past?

David Lawrence, editor of U.S. News and World Report, wrote: "The destiny of the world is in the hands of those statesmen who can interpret faithfully the commands of the Almighty."

Can our national leaders do this? Can they interpret faithfully the commands of the Almighty? Can we as citizens of this blessed land? Can we as people of the free world? Do we believe that "righteousness exalteth a nation," that there is safety only in righteous living?

Fortunately, today we are not left in darkness. We have guides—not only the Holy Bible, but added modern scriptures. And of the utmost importance for us today, we have the counsel and direction of living oracles. This counsel, this direction – in fact, the message of the fulness of the restored gospel – is being carried to the world by our missionaries, ambassadors of the Lord Jesus Christ.

And what is this message? It is a world message of the utmost importance. It is that God has again spoken from the heavens. The priesthood and authority to act in his name have been restored again to men on the earth, following centuries of darkness. The fulness of the everlasting gospel is here with all of its saving principles. To these facts I bear humble witness.

The prophets of a new gospel dispensation have counsel for us today – counsel on matters that concerned the founding fathers: freedom, liberty, righteousness which "exalteth a nation."

Do we believe and accept their counsel, or have we drifted away from those basic concepts and principles, without adherence to which, no nation can be exalted?

Elder Albert E. Bowen said:

"That which is right does not become wrong merely because it may be deserted by the majority, neither does that which is wrong today become right tomorrow by the chance circumstance that it has won the approval or been adopted by overwhelmingly predominant numbers. Principles cannot be changed by nor accommodate themselves to the vagaries of popular sentiment." (Conference Report, April 1941, p. 85.)

Modern-day prophets have said much by way of counsel and warning for our guidance. I turn to one who was called "a seer in the area of government" and who stood closest to the prophet of the Lord – the president of the Church – longer than any other man in Church history. I speak of President J. Reuben Clark, Jr.:

"There always comes a time when unpleasant truths must be retold, even though the retelling disturbs the ease and quiet of a luxurious error. Today seems to be such a time. On such occasions, the criticism, slander, misrepresentation that one gets, are of no consequence." (Address to Utah Wool Growers Association, January 24, 1945.)

"... today government has touched our lives so intimately in all their relationships and all these governmental touchings have been so tabbed as political, that we cannot discuss anything relating to our material welfare and existence without laying ourselves liable to the charge that we are talking politics." (Church News, June 16, 1945, p. 4.)

"I have been preaching against Communism for twenty years. I still warn you against it, and I tell you that we are drifting toward it more rapidly than some of us understand, and I tell you that when Communism comes, the ownership of the things which are necessary to feed your families is going to be taken away from us. I tell you freedom of speech will go, freedom of the press will go, and freedom of religion will go.

"I have warned you against propaganda and hate. We are in the midst of the greatest exhibition of propaganda that the world has ever seen, and all directed toward one end. Just do not believe all you read." (Conference Report, October 3, 1941, p. 16.)

"The plain and simple issue now facing us in America is freedom or slavery...

"Our real enemies are communism and its running mate, socialism...

"And never forget for one moment that communism and socialism are state slavery....

"... one thing seems sure, we will not get out of our present difficulties without trouble, serious trouble. Indeed, it may well be that our government and its free institutions will not be preserved except at the price of life and blood...

"... the paths we are following, if we move forward thereon, will inevitably lead us to socialism or communism, and these two are as like as two peas in a pod in their ultimate effect upon our liberties....

"We may first observe that communism and socialism – which we shall hereafter group together and dub Statism – cannot live with Christianity, nor with any religion that postulates a Creator such as the Declaration of Independence recognizes. The slaves of Statism must know no power, no authority, no source of blessing, no God, but the State...

"This country faces ahead enough trouble to bring us to our knees in humble honest prayer to God for the help which He alone can give, to save us...

"Do not think that all these usurpations, intimidations, and impositions are being done to us through inadvertency or mistake; the whole course is deliberately planned and carried out; its purpose is to destroy the Constitution and our Constitutional government...

"We have largely lost the conflict so far waged. But there is time to win the final victory, if we can sense our danger, and fight." (Church News, September 25, 1949, pp. 2, 15.)

Thus spoke the very forthright and courageous President J. Reuben Clark, Jr.

President David O. McKay said:

"During the first half of the twentieth century we have traveled far into the soul-destroying land of socialism and made strange alliances through which we have become involved in almost continuous hot and cold wars over the whole of the earth. In this retreat from freedom the voices of protesting citizens have been drowned by raucous shouts of intolerance and abuse from those who led the retreat and their millions of gullible youth, who are marching merrily to their doom, carrying banners on which are emblazoned such intriguing and misapplied labels as social justice, equality, reform, patriotism, social welfare." (Church News, October 18, 1952, p. 2.)

"The fostering of full economic freedom lies at the base of our liberties. Only in perpetuating economic freedom can our social, political, and religious liberties be preserved ... We must not let complacency blind our eyes to the real dangers threatening to destroy us." (Gospel Ideals, p. 433.)

"Communism is antagonistic to the American way of life. Its avowed purpose is to destroy belief in God and free enterprise. In education for citizenship, therefore, why should we not see to it that every child in America is taught the superiority of our way of life, of our Constitution and the sacredness of the freedom of the individual. Such definite instruction is not in violation of either the federal or the state constitution...

"I love the Stars and Stripes, and the American way of life. I have faith in the Constitution of the United States. I believe that only through a truly educated citizenry can the ideals that inspired the Founding Fathers of our nation be preserved." (Treasures of Life, pp. 501–503.)

Then President McKay listed as one of the four fundamental elements in such an education the "open and forceful teaching of facts regarding communism as an enemy to God and to individual freedom." (Ibid.)

At the opening session of the October 1961 semiannual general conference, President McKay gave a stirring address on our American way of life and the communist threat. He expressed grief and shock over a Supreme Court decision and stated that the enemies to our republican form of government are becoming more blatant.

At the close of the general conference in April 1962, President McKay emphasized that "men are rapidly classifying themselves into two groups: believers and nonbelievers." Then he quoted J. Edgar Hoover's warning:

"This nation is face to face with the greatest danger ever to confront it, a sinister and deadly conspiracy, which can be conquered only by an alert, informed citizenry. It is indeed appalling that some members of our society continue to deplore and criticize those who stress the communist danger. Public indifference to this threat is tantamount to national suicide. Lethargy leads only to disaster. Knowledge of the enemy, alertness to the danger, everyday patriotism are the brick and mortar with which we can build an impregnable fortress against communism." (Conference Report, April 1962, p. 125.)

In October 1962 President McKay said:
"In these days of uncertainty and unrest, liberty-loving people's greatest responsibility and paramount duty is to preserve and proclaim the freedom of the individual, his relationships to Deity, and the necessity of obedience to the principles of the gospel of Jesus Christ. Only thus will mankind find peace and happiness."

He concluded by urging Church members to "support good and conscientious candidates of either party who are aware of the great dangers inherent in communism, and who are truly dedicated to the Constitution in the tradition of the founding fathers." (Conference Report, October 1962, p. 8.)

We cannot say that the prophets of the Lord have not warned us. Do we heed their counsel? Are we in harmony? Every Latter-day Saint has spiritual obligations in four basic areas: his home, his church, his job, and his citizenship. Each of these areas should receive consistent attention, although not necessarily equal time. Are we doing our duty in these important fields? What about our citizenship responsibility – our obligation to safeguard our freedom and preserve the Constitution?

The Prophet Joseph Smith said the time would come when the Constitution would hang, as it were, by a thread. Modern-day prophets for the past several decades have been warning us that we have been rapidly moving in that direction. Fortunately, the Prophet Joseph Smith saw the part the elders of Israel would play in this crisis. Will there be some of us who won't care about saving the Constitution, others who will be blinded by the craftiness of men, and some who will knowingly be working to destroy it? He who has ears to hear and eyes to see can discern by the Spirit and through the words of God's mouthpiece that our liberties are being taken.

The enemy is amongst and upon us. Zion must awake and arouse herself. We, the elders of Israel, can be and should be the leaven in the loaf for freedom.

Years ago President Brigham Young stated:

"We all believe that the Lord will fight our battles; but how? Will he do it while we are unconcerned and make no effort whatever for our own safety when the enemy is upon us? ... it would be quite as reasonable to expect remission of sins without baptism, as to expect the Lord to fight our battles without our taking every precaution to be prepared to defend ourselves. The Lord requires us to be quite as willing to fight our own battles as to have Him fight them for us. If we are not ready for the enemy when he comes upon us, we have not lived up to the requirements of Him who guides the ship of Zion, or who dictates the affairs of His kingdom." (Journal of Discourses, vol. 11, p. 121.)

May we as a free people face courageously the challenging responsibility that faces us. "All that is necessary for the triumph of evil is that good men do nothing." (Edmund Burke.) We are not here to sit by complacently while our birthright of freedom is exchanged for a mess of socialist-communist pottage.

I love this great land – the Lord's Latter-day base of operations. I love the free world. I love our Father's children everywhere.

God bless us in our stewardship. May we be at least as valiant for freedom and righteousness, here and now, as we were when we fought for these principles in the preexistence. There is no other safe way, for "righteousness exalteth a nation."

GOD, FAMILY, COUNTRY

While attending the Fairfax Christian School in Virginia, my grandson Ezra Taft was introduced to the historical character Israel Putnam. Israel Putnam was one of the Revolutionary War farmers who left his plow in the field and gave up his comfort in order to protect his family, defend his inalienable God-given rights, and help establish this great, free country. It is heartening to know that today there are still those who answer to the rallying cry of God, family, and country.

Recently it was my privilege to walk across a part of that sacred soil where some of the best blood of Israel Putnam's generation was shed for freedom and the redemption of this land. Those noble souls did not initiate freedom, and one of the privileges of mortal life is the opportunity to rise in freedom's defense during the time when Lucifer is permitted to tempt and test men with his satanic schemes of slavery. This is part of our mission today. The same sun that shone on Israel Putnam during his mortal probation shines on us. And the same issues of light and darkness, force and freedom, right and wrong, that provided men a chance to prove themselves in his day continue to sift the souls of men today.

The thing that concerns so many of us today is not that wickedness is new, but that never before in our history has it been so well organized or so insidiously successful. Now, in view of this fact, and with a final showdown approaching between the powers of good and evil, may I be so bold as to make a few personal observations and express my convictions regarding God, family, and country.

I know, as I know that I live, that there is a God in heaven; that he is perfect and all powerful; that we are his children; that he loves us; and that we are eternal beings. I also know that life is a testing time in man's eternal existence, during which he is given his free agency – the right to choose between right and wrong – and that on those choices hang great consequences, not only in this life, but, even more important, in the life to come. There are boundaries beyond which Satan cannot go. Within those bounds, he is presently being permitted to offer an unrighteous alternative to God's righteous principles, thus allowing men to choose between good and evil and thereby determine the station they shall occupy in the next life. Said the poet:

Know this, that every soul is free
To choose his life and what he'll be,
For this eternal truth is given
That God will force no man to heaven.
He'll call, persuade, direct aright,
Bless with wisdom, love, and light;
In nameless ways be good and kind,
But never force the human mind.

God has not left man alone. He sends prophets, gives scripture, whispers counsel, answers righteous prayers, and in innumerable ways blesses his children. And he would more richly bless them if they were willing to obey the commands on which those blessings are predicated. I know that truth will eventually triumph and freedom will ultimately and finally prevail.

That fact alone should lift the spirit and hope of those who have an eternal view of things. Some of you will recall that during World War II, many of the British children were sent into rural areas for protection. One night, one of the small children, saying her prayers while the Battle of Britain raged over London, asked the Lord to bless the members of her family who were absent, including her father who was serving in the Royal Air Force. And as she was about to close her prayer, she said: "And dear God, please take care of yourself — because if anything happens to you, we're all sunk!"

Now, the great consolation and hope of every patriot should be that God is in his heaven; that he is the same yesterday, today, and forever; that this is his earth; that he is in charge; that his word will not fail; that in due time every wrong shall be righted, every virtue justified, every evil punished, and every good rewarded. But for the immediate future, we face times and calamities that will test the spiritual fiber of the best of us.

Now, with that knowledge, what is our responsibility? Why, what it has always been: to keep God's commandments. No more and no less. And that includes the declaration of Moses, inscribed on the Liberty Bell in Constitution Hall in Philadelphia, where the Declaration of Independence was signed: "Proclaim liberty throughout all the land, unto all the inhabitants thereof." (Lev. 25:10.)

It is my conviction that despite the serious trials and tribulations we will have to face before Jehovah's triumphal return, the forces of freedom and righteousness, which have never been better organized than they are today, shall not be destroyed. The number who are dedicated to, and will preserve, our inspired Constitution are on the increase, and God watches over the faithful no matter what is going on in the world.

It is our duty to be faithful, and a man cannot be counted among the fully faithful unless he is an active fighter for freedom. Resistance to tyranny is still obedience to God. How to resist in the most effective manner will require careful and prayerful thought on the part of all of us. To be fully effective in the fight for freedom, a man must be in tune with the greatest champion and leader of free men — the Lord our God. And to be in tune with him, we must be in step with him; we must walk in his way.

Now, that divine duty to be a faithful fighter for freedom requires that those of us who have been warned do our duty to warn our neighbor, for our neighbor's involvement in this struggle can bless his soul, strengthen his family, and protect him from pitfalls while he helps his country. The blessings far outweigh the burden when we stand up for freedom. With gall comes glory; with a cross comes a crown; with thorns comes a throne, if we will persevere in righteousness. There are still more victories to be won in this fight for freedom, the most important of which is to save our own souls by taking a stand for liberty with the Lord. For amid the encircling gloom, the kindly light of the Lord can lead us on – can help expose and stop evil in some places, slow it down in others, give the forces of freedom the chance to become better entrenched, provide righteous alternatives, and develop faith and hope to keep on keeping on in the divine assurance that in the brightness of the Lord's coming, the darkness of Satan's conspiracy will eventually be fully exposed and destroyed.

Now, in preparation for the showdown, may I encourage each of us to strengthen our families. The communists are determined to destroy the three great loyalties – loyalty to God, loyalty to family, and loyalty to country. Some of our patriots are losing their children. In our attempt to save our country, we must not let our own homes crumble. Don't neglect your own. You can't delegate that divine duty nor neglect it without tragic consequences. be careful in sending them away from your hearth for additional education. There are worse things that can happen to a young person today than not getting a liberal college degree.

We must multiply our influence by raising up God-fearing patriots at our own fireside. We need more than one generation of patriots in a family line. We need more men like John Adams, who took time amid all the demands of the revolution and the building of this republic to teach and train a future president, his own son, John Quincy Adams. We must stay close to our children.

Not only should we have strong spiritual homes, but we should have strong temporal homes. We should avoid bondage by getting out of debt as soon as we can, pay as we go, and live within our incomes. There is wisdom in having on hand a year's supply of food, clothing, and fuel, if possible, and in being prepared to defend our families and our possessions and to take care of ourselves. I believe a man should prepare for the worst while working for the best. Some people prepare and don't work, while others work but don't prepare. Both are needed if we would be of maximum service to our God, our family, and our country.

It is a part of my religious belief that America is a land choice above all others, that we are not just another of the family of nations, but that we have been singled out to perform a divine mission for liberty-loving people everywhere. Those who founded this republic were wise men raised up by our Father in heaven to perform that very task, and the Constitution of this land was inspired by God. We have a divine duty – even a destiny – to preserve that Constitution from destruction and hold it aloft to the world.

A book that I accept as scripture tells of two ancient American civilizations that were destroyed as a result of murderous conspiracies lusting for power and seeking to overthrow freedom. That book warned that when we should see a similar situation developing in our land in our day, we would be under commandment of the Lord to awake to our awful situation. That day is upon us, and those of us who are awake to our situation have a moral obligation to do all we can to awaken our fellow citizens.

The Book of Mormon states that America will remain a free land as long as the people worship the God of the land. It also assures us that "unto the righteous" this land "shall be blessed forever."

I remember a number of years ago when Cecil B. DeMille, the great producer of such films as The Ten Commandments, was invited to accept an honorary degree from Brigham Young University. In his address to the student body, Mr. DeMille made an interesting observation. He said that men and nations cannot really break the Ten Commandments; they can only break themselves upon them. How true!

And so, in talking about our country as well as our families, we return again to God, because this whole basic struggle revolves around the spiritual and moral fitness of our people. Nineveh was saved because the people repented while there was still time. But Sodom was destroyed because God couldn't find even ten worthy souls. As the wicked become more wicked and more numerous, the righteous will need to increase in spiritual strength and numbers to offset them. One of the great blessings of the last few years is that the patriotic movement in America has become organized and strengthened to an unprecedented degree.

A while ago some lonely American must have felt like Elijah, who fled into the wilderness thinking that he was alone in rejecting false gods. But God knew differently and told Elijah of some 7,000 who had not bent their knees to the idols. This lifted Elijah's heart and he went back to the battle with Baal. We know that we are not alone in this freedom fight. Many have helped lift other hearts, but there are many more who feel alone whose knees have not bent or who might be wobbly. There may be some who, with our help, understanding, and encouragement, might get off their knees to the idol of socialism and acquit themselves like men.

We must have an even greater determination to reach and influence those who, with our help, understanding, and encouragement, might themselves join us in the battle. God is counting on us to follow through. If we do it well, then we will have done our job. Like the watchman on the tower referred to in the Bible, it is our task to warn others of the darkness. Some will not listen, and they will be held accountable. But if we who have the word fail to issue the warning, then God will hold us accountable.

May we pledge anew that the divine principles embodied in the divinely inspired documents that govern our country be written on the tablets of our own hearts. I pray that our eyes might be single to the will of God, that we might thereby bless our families and our country, and that we shall, with increased devotion, work for less government, more individual responsibility, and, with God's help, a better world.

I TESTIFY

My beloved brethren and sisters, my heart is full and my feelings tender as we conclude this great general conference of the Church.

We have been richly blessed as we have listened to the counsel and testimonies of those who have spoken to us.

As a special witness of Jesus Christ, and as His humble servant, it is now my obligation and privilege, as the Spirit dictates, to bear pure testimony and witness to that which I know to be true. (See Alma 4:19.) This I will do.

I testify that we are the spirit offspring of a loving God, our Heavenly Father (see Acts 17:29; 1 Ne. 17:36). He has a great plan of salvation whereby His children might be perfected as He is and might have a fulness of joy as He enjoys. (See 1 Ne. 10:18; 2 Ne. 2:25; Alma 24:14; Alma 34:9; 3 Ne. 12:48; 3 Ne. 28:10.)

I testify that in our premortal state our Elder Brother in the spirit, even Jesus Christ, became our foreordained Savior in the Father's plan of salvation. (See Mosiah 4:6–7; Alma 34:9.) He is the captain of our salvation and the only means through whom we can return to our Father in Heaven to gain that fulness of joy. (See Heb. 2:10; Mosiah 3:17; Alma 38:9.)

I testify that Lucifer was also in the council of heaven. He sought to destroy the agency of man. He rebelled. (See Moses 4:3.) There was a war in heaven, and a third of the hosts were cast to the earth and denied a body. (See Rev. 12:7–9; D&C 29:36–37.) Lucifer is the enemy of all righteousness and seeks the misery of all mankind. (See 2 Ne. 2:18, 27; Mosiah 4:14.)

I testify that all those who come into mortality accepted our Father's plan. (See Abr. 3:26.) Having proved faithful in their first estate in heaven, they are now subject to the test of mortality in this second estate. That test entails doing all things whatsoever the Lord requires. (See Abr. 3:25.) Those who prove faithful in this second estate will have glory added upon their heads forever and ever. (See Abr. 3:26.)

I testify that God reveals His will to all men through the Light of Christ. (See Moro. 7:16; D&C 93:2; John 1:9.) They receive the additional light of the gift of the Holy Ghost through the laying on of hands by God's authorized servants following baptism. (See A of F 1:4; D&C 20:41.)

I testify that throughout the ages God has spoken to His children through His prophets. (See Amos 3:7; Hel. 8:13–20.) Only when His children rejected the prophets were the prophets taken out of their midst, and then tragedy followed. (See 1 Ne. 3:17–18; 1 Ne. 7:14; Hel. 13:24–27.)

I testify that Christ was born into mortality with Mary as His mother and our Heavenly Father as His father. (See 1 Ne. 11:18–21; Mosiah 3:8.) He lived a sinless life, providing us a perfect example. (See D&C 45:4; 3 Ne. 12:48; 3 Ne. 27:27.) He worked out the great Atonement, which, through His grace, provides for every soul a resurrection and, for the faithful, the means to become exalted in the celestial kingdom. (See A of F 1:3; 2 Ne. 25:23; Mosiah 4:6–7; Alma 11:41–45; D&C 76:50–70; D&C 132:19.)

I testify that during His mortal ministry Christ established His church on the earth. (See Matt. 16:18; Acts 2:47; 3 Ne. 21:22.) He called and ordained men to be Apostles and prophets with authority so that what they bound on earth would be bound in heaven. (See Matt. 16:19; John 15:16.) They received revelation, which provided new scripture. (See 2 Pet. 1:20–21; D&C 68:4.)

I testify that a world so wicked that it killed the Son of God soon began killing the Apostles and prophets and so plunged itself into a spiritual dark age. (See 2 Thes. 2:2–7.) Scripture ended, apostasy spread, and the church that Christ established during His earthly ministry ceased to exist. (See 2 Ne. 27:4–5.)

I testify that God the Father and His Son, Jesus Christ, appeared to Joseph Smith in the spring of 1820, thus bringing to an end the long night of apostasy (JS–H 1:15–20). To Joseph Smith appeared other beings, including John the Baptist and Peter, James, and John, who ordained him with authority to act in the name of God (see JS–H 1:68–72; D&C 27:5–13). The church and kingdom of God was restored in these latter days, even The Church of Jesus Christ of Latter-day Saints, with all the gifts, rights, powers, doctrines, officers, and blessings of the former-day Church. (See D&C 65; D&C 115:3–4.)

I testify that through the Book of Mormon God has provided for our day tangible evidence that Jesus is the Christ and that Joseph Smith is His prophet. (See D&C 20:8–33.) This other testament of Jesus Christ is a scriptural account of the early inhabitants of America. It was translated by Joseph Smith through the gift and power of God. (See D&C 135:3.) Those who will read and ponder the Book of Mormon and ask our Eternal Father in the name of Christ if it is true may know for themselves of its truthfulness through the power of the Holy Ghost, provided they will ask with a sincere heart, with real intent, having faith in Christ. (See Moro. 10:3–5.)

I testify that America is a choice land. (See 2 Ne. 1:5.) God raised up the founding fathers of the United States of America and established the inspired Constitution. (See D&C 101:77–80.) This was the required prologue for the restoration of the gospel. (See 3 Ne. 21:4.) America will be a blessed land unto the righteous forever and is the base from which God will continue to direct the worldwide Latter-day operations of His kingdom. (See 2 Ne. 1:7.)

I testify that there has been, and there is now, and there will be legal successors to the Prophet Joseph Smith who hold the keys of the kingdom of God on earth, even the President of The Church of Jesus

Christ of Latter-day Saints. (See D&C 21:1–7; D&C 107:91–92; D&C 112:15.) He receives revelation from God to direct His kingdom. Associated with him are others who are prophets, seers, and revelators, even those who make up the presiding quorums of the Church, namely the First Presidency and the Quorum of the Twelve Apostles. (See D&C 112:30.)

I testify that wickedness is rapidly expanding in every segment of our society. (See D&C 1:14–16; D&C 84:49–53.) It is more highly organized, more cleverly disguised, and more powerfully promoted than ever before. Secret combinations lusting for power, gain, and glory are flourishing. A secret combination that seeks to overthrow the freedom of all lands, nations, and countries is increasing its evil influence and control over America and the entire world. (See Ether 8:18–25.)

I testify that the church and kingdom of God is increasing in strength. Its numbers are growing, as is the faithfulness of its faithful members. It has never been better organized or equipped to perform its divine mission.

I testify that as the forces of evil increase under Lucifer's leadership and as the forces of good increase under the leadership of Jesus Christ, there will be growing battles between the two until the final confrontation. As the issues become clearer and more obvious, all mankind will eventually be required to align themselves either for the kingdom of God or for the kingdom of the devil. As these conflicts rage, either secretly or openly, the righteous will be tested. God's wrath will soon shake the nations of the earth and will be poured out on the wicked without measure. (See JS–H 1:45; D&C 1:9.) But God will provide strength for the righteous and the means of escape; and eventually and finally truth will triumph. (See 1 Ne. 22:15–23.)

I testify that it is time for every man to set in order his own house both temporally and spiritually. It is time for the unbeliever to learn for himself that this work is true, that The Church of Jesus Christ of Latter-day Saints is the kingdom which Daniel prophesied God would set up in the latter days, never to be destroyed, a stone that would eventually fill the whole earth and stand forever. (See Dan. 2:34–45;

D&C 65:2.) It is time for us, as members of the Church, to walk in all the ways of the Lord, to use our influence to make popular that which is sound and to make unpopular that which is unsound. We have the scriptures, the prophets, and the gift of the Holy Ghost. Now we need eyes that will see, ears that will hear, and hearts that will hearken to God's direction.

I testify that not many years hence the earth will be cleansed. (See D&C 76:41.) Jesus the Christ will come again, this time in power and great glory to vanquish His foes and to rule and reign on the earth. (See D&C 43:26–33.) In due time all men will gain a resurrection and then will face the Master in a final judgment. (See 2 Ne. 9:15, 41.) God will give rewards to each according to the deeds done in the flesh. (See Alma 5:15.)

I testify to you that a fulness of joy can only come through the atonement of Jesus Christ and by obedience to all of the laws and ordinances of the gospel, which are found only in The Church of Jesus Christ of Latter-day Saints. (See A of F 1:3.)

To all these things I humbly testify and bear my solemn witness that they are true, and I do so in the name of Him who is the head of this church, even Jesus Christ, amen.

APPENDIX
Sources of Material Used

1. "My People Are Destroyed for Lack of Knowledge." General conference address, April 1960.

2. "A Plea to Strengthen Our Families." General conference address, October 1970.

3. "The Book of Mormon Is the Word of God." General conference address, April 1975.

4. "Beware of Pride." General conference address, April 1989.

5. "The Twelfth Article of Faith." Article in the *Instructor*, December 1955, pp. 332-333.

6. "The Constitution: A Heavenly Banner". Address delivered at the Marriott Center, September 16, 1986.

7. "Stand Up For Freedom." Address delivered at the Utah Forum for the American Ideal, Assembly Hall at Temple Square, Feb 11, 1966.

8. "The Proper Role of Government." Address delivered at the Utah Forum for the American Ideal, Salt Lake City, Utah, February 29, 1968.

9. "Civic Standards for the Faithful Saints." General conference address, April 6, 1972.

10. "United States Foreign Policy." Address delivered at the Farm Bureau Banquet, Preston Idaho, June 21, 1968.

11. "Freedom and Free Enterprise." Circa 1977.

12. "Our Immediate Responsibility." Address delivered at BYU Devotional, October 25, 1966.

13. "Christ and the Constitution." General conference address, April 8, 1967.

14. "Be Not Deceived." General conference address, October 1963.

15. "Watchman, Warn The Wicked." General conference address, April 6, 1973.

16. "Not Commanded in All Things." General conference address, April 5, 1965.

17. "Righteousness Exalteth a Nation." General conference address, April 7, 1963.

18. "God, Family, Country." Address delivered at the New England Rally for God, Family, and Country honor banquet, Boston, Massachusetts, July 4, 1972.

19. "I Testify." General conference address, October 1988.

ABOUT THE AUTHOR

Ezra Taft Benson (1899 – 1994) was called to be an Apostle in 1943. He served as U.S. Secretary of Agriculture from 1953 to 1961. On November 10, 1985, he became President of The Church of Jesus Christ of Latter-day Saints. Among the most notable of Ezra Taft Benson's accomplishments are his promotion of the principles of liberty and the proper role of government, his testimony of the Book of Mormon, and commitment in leading souls to Christ through the Gospel.

Made in the USA
Columbia, SC
27 May 2021